Angels in Action

EMAN.ᴸ SWEDENBORG

Angels in Action

WHAT SWEDENBORG

SAW AND HEARD

Robert H. Kirven

Chrysalis Books
Imprint of the Swedenborg Foundation
West Chester, Pennsylvania

Chrysalis Books is an imprint of the Swedenborg Foundation, Inc. For more information, contact:
Chrysalis Books
Swedenborg Foundation
320 N. Church Street
West Chester, PA 19380

Library of Congress Cataloging-in-Publication Data

Kirven, Robert H.
    Angels in action : what Swedenborg saw and heard / Robert H. Kirven
       p.   cm.
    ISBN 0-87785-147-6 (pbk.)
    1. Angels. 2. Swedenborg, Emanuel, 1688-1772—Views on angels.
I. Title
BX8729.A54K57   1994   94-30945
235'.3—dc20   CIP

Edited by Stuart Shotwell
Designed by Joanna V. Hill
Cover art by John Flaxman. Reproduced by permission of Musées départementaux de Loire-Atlantique, Musée Dobrée, Nantes, France

Typeset in Sabon and Cochin by Ruttle, Shaw, & Wetherill, Inc.
Printed and bound by BookCrafters

Contents

List of Illustrations / *vii*
About the Artist / viii

Preface / *xi*

1. What Angels Do / *3*
Angels Help People Die / 4
Angels Help Infants / 8
Angels Help People Find the Way / 11
Angels Help People Celebrate / 16

2. Angels and Spirits / *21*
Evil Spirits / 24
The Battleground / 30
Spirits Becoming Angels / 36

3. Who Says So? / *41*
The Man / 41
The Message / 48
Can You Believe It? / 54

4. What He Said / *59*

Human Nature / 59

People, Spirits, and Angels / 64

How Angels Live / 68

Love and Marriage among the Angels / 73

5. Freedom / *77*

False and Evil Influences / 79

Equilibrium / 82

Guardian Angels / 84

Whom Do We Trust? / 90

Who's in Charge? / 94

6. What We Can Do / *97*

We Can Help People / 98

We Can Keep in Touch / 105

We Can Help the Angels / 108

Illustrations

All illustrations in the text, unless otherwise noted, are pen and pencil drawings by John Flaxman and are used with permission of the Henry E. Huntington Library and Art Gallery, San Marino, California. The numbers following the titles refer to the Huntington catalog.

Drawing of an Angel with Children, no. 68 / i and 1

Emanuel Swedenborg, taken from *A Treatise concerning Heaven and Hell* . . ., printed by Cowdroy & Slack, Bury-Street, 1812 / ii

John Flaxman, Self-portrait, 1779, reproduced with permission of College Art Collections, University College, London / ix

Design for monument of Sophia Hoare, no. 38 / 5

Drawing of an Angel with Children, no. 69 / 9

Know Ye Not to Whom Ye Yield Yourselves, no. 29 / 25

Design for monument of Mrs. Frances Schutz Drury Hawkins, no. 39 / 37

Emanuel Swedenborg, engraved by Johann-Martin Bernigeroth as frontispiece to *Principia*, 1734, from the Image Archives of the Swedenborg Foundation / 42

Angels Descending to the Daughters of Men, no. 25 / 49

Aspects of the Human Spirit, by R. H. Kirven / 61

Frieze of Classical Figures, no. 51 / 63

Illustration to *Paradise Lost*, no. 19 / 74

She Thought She Saw Two Ill-favored Ones, no. 21 / 80

A Pediment Representing the Sciences, no. 48 / 83

Two Figures Watching over a Sleeping Man, reproduced by
  permission of Musées départementaux de Loire-
  Atlantique, Musée Dobrée, Nantes, France / 85

Mother and Child and Group of Four Children,
  no. 4 / 91

Pestilence, no. 24 / 95

Design for monument of Thomas Yarborough and His
  Family, no. 35 / 100

Four Girls Reading, no. 73 / 107

Design for Candelabrum Representing Mercury Presenting
  the Infant Bacchus to the Nymphs, no. 60 / 109

A Grecian Woman Seated beside a Pedestal and a Bush,
  no. 75 / 112

About the Artist

John Flaxman (1755-1826) was an influential artist at the turn of the nineteenth century and one of England's leading proponents of neoclassical art. Flaxman started his career working with Josiah Wedgwood and was responsible for many of the neoclassical designs on Wedgwood's popular two-toned Jasperware. At the height of his career, he was made a member of the Royal Academy and was the first professor of sculpture for that institution.

Flaxman's early reputation was established as an engraver, but in later years he was also well known as a sculptor of funerary monuments. It has been pointed out that

John Flaxman, Self-portrait, 1779

Flaxman's monuments display unique elements, the source of which can be traced back to his reading of Emanuel Swedenborg. For example, Flaxman depicts the soul as fully embodied, with distinctly masculine or feminine characteristics; and the body as rising immediately after death, not on a judgment day sometime in the future.

Flaxman was indeed an avid reader of Swedenborg. He attended the first public meeting about Swedenborg and later joined a Swedenborgian congregation. Even though he left the established church after a time, he remained an admirer of the Swedish seer and associated with other readers of Swedenborg, such as William Blake and Samuel Taylor Coleridge. Flaxman also supported a nonsectarian society dedicated to publishing Swedenborg's works, which later became the Swedenborg Society.

One of the most interesting aspects of the artist's work is a group of drawings he did illustrating Swedenborg's *Arcana Coelestia*. Since Swedenborg teaches that all angels were once human beings, Flaxman depicts them without wings. Further, these angels are not mourning over the dead but are quietly waiting for the soul to become conscious in the spiritual world.

Those interested in learning more about Flaxman's career may consult David Irwin's biography, *John Flaxman 1755-1826* (London: Studio Vista/Christie's, 1979).

MARTHA GYLLENHEAL

Bryn Athyn, Pennsylvania

Preface

Angels are all around us. There can be no doubt about it. Even if you doubt or deny their actual existence, you cannot escape their conspicuous presence in popular movies, best-selling books, prime-time television series, major weekly newsmagazines, and other sources. Angels are all around us.

With so many angels all over the place, why another book on angels? What more needs to be said?

Some writers, curious about angels, have researched the relevant literature and published summaries and analyses of it. Other people have seen or had an experience with angels, or talked to people who have, and written about that. But one observer, Emanuel Swedenborg, spent more than twenty-seven years in almost daily conversation and activity with angels and other spirits. Although he wrote a lot about angels—there are references to angels in all the thirty volumes of the English translation of his theological works—there has been no single book telling just what he said about angels and what they do. This book fills that gap.

On a more personal level, I have been learning about angels, and about Swedenborg, for most of my three-score-years and going-on-ten, and what I have learned has helped me live my life as successfully as—or no more unsuccessfully than—I have. Knowledge about angels and the ways that they affect people has been invaluable to me, so I would like to share these insights.

For thirty years as an educator, I taught people about Swedenborg, about his ideas, and about the history of Christian thought. I had the opportunity and good fortune to become familiar with details of what Swedenborg wrote about angels. But I also remember an earlier time in my life, when I had questions I could not answer, questions about Swedenborg, questions about God, that led me to distance myself from churches for a while. These memories give me deep empathy for those who ask "Who says so?" and "How do you know?"

Questioners who have doubts about the relevance to their lives of the Bible, or of churches, or of the vocabulary of Christian concerns are invited to suspend judgment on those issues until they have read more about what angels do in the lives of people of every religion and of no religion.

The organization of the book is straightforward. On the presumption that readers would prefer reading something about angels in action before learning details about Swedenborg, the first chapter describes angels and some of the things they do. However, readers who first want to learn more about my fundamental source of information will find it in chapter 3, "Who Says So?"

Much of what is said about angels in the first chapter refers to spirits as well, but Swedenborg distinguished between the two types of beings. The connection that he made between angels and spirits is described at the beginning of chapter 2, "Angels and Spirits."

Both the Swedenborgian background and my own life experience have convinced me that information about the actions of angels in our lives can be useful to anyone. My prayerful hope is that this book will help readers become more sensitive to the spiritual support available from the angels. Some readers, no doubt, may have difficulty accepting or verifying angelic activity. The discussion of Swedenborg's insights is intended to help in this regard. I can add that after living with these insights for many years, I have found their internal consistency and harmony with the rest I know of life to be strongly self-validating. See what you think.

In closing, I want to express my appreciation to Bill, Dave, Don, George, John, Nancy, and other angels—most with bodies, but some without—who helped me write this book.

Angels in Action

1. What Angels Do

It might be argued that a description of what angels do should be preceded by a demonstration that angels are real. But the most convincing evidence for the reality of angels is the realization that something that has happened in one's own life is the work of an angel. After all, only a real being can really do something. A description of angelic activity may trigger a response, whether a memory or an intuition, that can confirm the reality of angels more forcefully than logical reasoning.

Angels ordinarily are in action. They do not sit around on clouds, or thrones, or anything else, as we often see them in some art and cartoons. Except for periods of rest, comparable to our sleeping at night, they do not sit around at all. Instead, they are busy at what they love to do. That includes worshipping, teaching or learning, serving God, enjoying recreation, assisting one another, and helping people in this world. Most real angels are not preoccupied with the people and circumstances that they left behind in the physical world; and the aid they give people is spiritual, rather than material. They help people like you and me find the way, or gain the strength, or learn the patience, or find the courage to do what needs to be done. They are not "free agents" who choose whom they will help: they are messengers or agents of God, carrying out God's will and embodying divine mercy.

A clear picture of how angels assist people requires an understanding of how our lives mesh with the activity of angels and other spirits. We will get to that explanation. But by way of introduction, we will look first at a kind of aid that angels give people that is easy to imagine.

Angels Help People Die

When people die—or, more accurately, when their physical bodies die—angels with special inclination and training for this work instantaneously are present to help them make the transition from bodily life to entirely spiritual life.

Usually, this assistance is invisible to the physical eyes of professionals and loved ones near the dying person. Sometimes, however, people who are especially open to angelic aid will react to it while their spirit still activates their body. When this happens, the dying person often says or does things that are incomprehensible to observers who are not aware that angelic helpers are present at the time of death.

A friend of mine who knew about angels, though he did not speak of them often, passed into a coma at the onset of a massive and fatal heart attack. Lying unconscious on the floor while his wife watched for the ambulance, he spoke the last words of his physical existence: "Yes, I understand what you're trying to do."

He was speaking to the angels who were helping him get ready for the separation of his spirit from his body. He already knew what is known by most people who have sur-

Angels reassure us as we enter our next life.

vived near-death experiences or spiritual experiences of other kinds: a person continues to live after the body dies. So he may not have been surprised to find angels around him, like medical attendants preparing to detach a patient from a heart-lung machine, only with more wise and sensitive care for the many processes taking place. Most people need help at that point. After all, few arrive at it with any relevant experience. Moreover, the process presents difficulties for many people because it requires dissolving all the intricate, intimate bonds we have with our body and its environment, and opening our mind and senses to a whole range of influences and sensations of which we never before have been consciously aware.

A woman who became a close friend of mine some time ago, in spite of her being older than my parents, enjoyed a long marriage during which she and her husband grew so much alike that they came to look more like siblings than like spouses. She outlived her husband by a few years, and mentioned in the course of one conversation after his death that she spoke with him every night. While I had no doubt about the continuation of life after physical death, her statement did make me wonder if my friend was slipping into a state of senility.

After her death a few months later, however, I came to see her comment in a different light. She had been asleep, according to a mutual friend who had been by her bedside at the time. On awaking, she looked around, and her face suddenly brightened with a smile of happy recognition. Seeing someone whom our mutual friend could not, she spoke her late husband's name: "Malcolm!" More animated than she had been for days or weeks, she continued, "Is it time, at last?" I assume she received an affirmative reply, because she closed her eyes and, still smiling, leaned back against the pillow and died. She was thoroughly prepared, as well as pleased, to rejoin her husband and continue their relationship. It seemed natural to her that he would welcome her, even before her body had finished dying—and on reflection it seemed natural to me, too.

On the other hand, people who are particularly unprepared for their transition to completely spiritual life—either because they die suddenly, or do not expect to live after death, or for some other reason—need special help with the process. Some people who have come near death have described moving through a "tunnel" to where kind and loving care is offered. Emanuel Swedenborg, the eighteenth-century

Swedish scientist and mystic who wrote extensively about angels, tells of being given a demonstration of a typical withdrawal from the body transition to a completely spiritual life. His account describes how he first encountered some of the kindest and most profoundly loving of all angels close beside him, two near his heart and two by his head. It also explains how people "wake up" gradually after dying, first becoming aware of the angels near the head. These angels care much more deeply and perceptively than human beings do, so their thoughts are too loving for people fresh from this life to understand a word they say. Speaking is not necessary, however. Their radiant love makes their very presence so comforting, and makes their faces so expressive, that they are able to communicate everything that is needed to make someone who has just died feel safe and welcome and at peace. Other angels, closer to the heart, are noticed next. They, too, naturally would speak in ways the new spirit could not understand; but they change their speech so as to be understood as they answer the spirit's first befuddled questions, carefully and lovingly explaining the person's new situation.

After new arrivals are able to accept their changed situation—and many do, immediately, with little or no help—they begin to meet angelic spirits more like themselves. If they are confused about what is happening, they may be visited first by teachers who are especially adept at explaining the transition. Or, as frequently happens, they first meet spouses who have died before them, or their parents, other relatives, or close friends from their life in this world. These meetings reinforce the knowledge that their physical body actually has died (for they doubt it, since they feel so real and substantial), or that life continues after death (if they doubt that); but their greater purpose is to provide these angelic friends with opportunities to aid newcomers in adjusting to their new life.

Angels do this in the most natural ways. By simply looking, sounding, and acting like people who normally might be met in the physical world (after all, they once were humans), they exert a reassuring presence. By talking about experiences that angels and human spirits have shared, they establish trust. And, as needed, they explain more things about the newcomer's new life.

There is, indeed, much to learn and understand. New arrivals need to realize what it is they really cherish and most want to do, as opposed to the things they have done in the physical world because they had to, or because they felt they would gain some profit or respect. After realizing what kind of spirit they really are, beneath all pretense and appearance, they must find a spiritual community with similar goals and preferences; and then they have a lot to learn about differences between what they believed and "knew," and the realities of life in the spiritual world. There are angels to assist them with every aspect of this process.

Angels Help Infants

One reason that dying people can accept the deep and comforting affection of angels so readily is that their radiantly loving presence awakens a subconscious memory from earliest childhood. All children are closely accompanied by angels from the moment of their birth through the first months of

Angels especially love children.

life. Angelic and spiritual company continues after this, as well, but in a different way. During the initial months of life—approximately until the child is weaned—the child is unable to make any choices, and, therefore, is not yet involved in the conflict between good and evil influences. During this innocent period, angels with a particular love for babies stay close to the infants, sharing their love, providing them with spiritual protection, and making sure that they start life with an inner experience of what is true and good.

This early experience of angelic love and wisdom is vitally important in every person's life. Although they do not rise to consciousness, our feelings in response to that angelic care and instruction remain in our subliminal memory. That is the reason that people can recognize love and goodness, truth and beauty, later in life—no matter how deprived or repressed their physical life may have been.

The innocence of infants, which keeps them open to angelic care and companionship, is a priceless human quality. It is gradually lost in the child's necessary development, because growing up requires a sense of self-confidence, ownership and responsibility, self-worth, and self-discipline. However, people who grow wise when they get older regain something very much like an infant's innocence—namely, a new perspective on themselves and their place in the world—which can be called the innocence of wisdom.

The innocence of infants attracts the concern and care of angels who are good enough and strong enough to protect infants from all kinds of evil or harmful spiritual influences. Some of these angels who gather around infants have achieved such a high degree of the innocence of wisdom in themselves that they look like children to other angels except that everyone in heaven knows that angels who look like infants are among the wisest and most blessed and powerful.

Spiritual protection of infants is typical of angelic occupations in that it is a kind of service. It is one of the joys of heavenly life that every angel is able to do good things for others in a manner that requires them to engage in the activity that they most love. For example, angels who have a special affection for newborn children are the ones who have the task of caring for them.

Other angels and spirits replace these earliest guardians when infants begin to mature. As children gradually perceive the distinctions that require them to make choices, their sense of self—which also is a necessary part of decision making—displaces more and more of the innocence in which they were born, and they need spiritual guidance and support more than protection. Spiritual companionship and surroundings continue to change throughout the individual's development, always mirroring one's values and goals.

Angels Help People Find the Way

Angels and angelic spirits serve us in many other ways during our life before death. When we need more strength or courage or clearer direction than we feel we have within ourselves, our appeals for help—our silent or spoken prayers—bring angelic assistance if those appeals are genuine and if we are willing to accept help. Angels are sent to us when we need to be led away from evil desires and the thoughts that spring from them. When they succeed with such leading, they then attempt to inspire us with good affections, so that we will intend and accomplish things that improve our human communities.

Most frequently, the support or guidance comes through spiritual depths that lie beneath our consciousness: when we become aware of them the strength or direction seems to have come from within—from some previously unknown resource. Sometimes, when that kind of assistance does not meet the need, angels approach us in dreams, in hypnagogic states (the condition between sleeping and waking, which also can be induced by meditative practice), or even in fully awakened consciousness.

When angels speak to us, it is not in their own language (as was mentioned earlier), for we can neither hear nor understand their speech. Instead, they communicate with subconscious elements of our minds, where thoughts are formed that are then turned into words. In this process, when the idea they have communicated reaches our consciousness, we think it in words of our native tongue or another language that we know well.

Sometimes, spiritual communication can be heard by a person as a voice. When that happens, however, the thought comes through our unconscious mind, is formed into verbal thoughts that we seem to hear, so that it is hard to tell whether the sound came from within or without.

Far more often than angels speak words to us, however, they communicate desires, values, or other affections. When you see or imagine a thing or an action and feel a strong desire or approval—or, on the other hand, a strong distaste or disapproval—that is precisely the kind of feeling angels communicate most often. The glow of affirmation, almost physically warm, when a line of a hymn you are singing in church expresses a truth about your life is a common example of this. So, too, is the emotion behind the involuntary blush of shame that makes poor liars of so many of us.

How do we know whether such a feeling originates with us or is inspired by an angel? There is no easy way to distinguish with certainty between an emotion that is felt deeply and a feeling induced by angelic influence. However, when your reaction is surprising to you, perhaps unlike your customary response, you may very well be experiencing a spiritual encouragement to correct your first inclination. When "nudges" of this kind do not provide the help you need and seek, angels can communicate thoughts, and feelings about those thoughts, through mental images. On occasion, the images can even include words.

One such event, clear in my memory almost fifty years after it happened, occurred during the late years of the European phase of World War II. In retrospect, it is clear that Allied victory was growing near; but to my depressed mind, American defeat seemed a frighteningly real possibility. This prospect, which I now know was encouraged if not originated by evil spirits, was invading my consciousness enough to interfere with my college studies. Then one night I dreamed that I was standing in an open field. There was no person or building in sight, just me, standing before a massive tangle of coiled barbed wire that stretched to the horizon on my left and on my right, fencing me in. As I stood there, an angel, appearing as a light too bright to look at, came over the hill ahead of me, leaving a paved highway in its wake. It approached me, passing through the barbed wire, which vaporized before it, and then passed by and moved on out of sight behind me. Realizing I was free, I walked forward on the road in the direction from which the angel had come. I woke. My obsession with the war, and my general depression, was lifted from that time on. The angel had saved me from the irrational fear that had held me captive. Even without words, the communication was clear. My experiential certainty that angels can do such things has helped me break free from other fears as well.

Another time, a couple of decades later, I found myself confused and frustrated over possible career choices. I had abandoned a promising career in one field, enrolled in graduate school to prepare for another, and had reached a point at which I could feel no sense of direction or purpose. Again it was night, but this time I had just awakened from a dream of walking alone, along deserted streets of a city that I would have thought was New York had it not been empty of any sign of life.

Awake, but still visualizing the street, I imagined myself continuing to walk along it. Without "deciding" to do so, I tried the knob of a door, found it open, and walked through it. Ahead of me was a staircase winding downward, and I started walking down. After descending several floors, I imagined that I was now tired of walking and had stepped off into the middle of the stairwell. I fell for a long time and finally landed unhurt at the bottom. There I saw a light coming from an arched stone doorway and entered the room from which the light came.

It was a circular, stone-walled room, with an arched window looking down on green hills dotted with trees of the sort that might be drawn by a child—brown trunks topped by green balls of foliage with orange balls in them representing fruit. Looking around the room, I saw a robed and hooded monk, his back to me, writing with a quill pen at a desk. This monk, I realized then, was an angel who knew all my problems and potentials. Though not sure at first of what to say, I eventually asked, "Who are you?" The figure did not answer or turn toward me, but after a moment the hooded robe sank to the floor, empty. Presently it rose again, and I realized that I was standing in the robe, with the pen in my hand.

Picking up a pencil and paper from beside the bed, I wrote as well as I could without opening my eyes (it was dark, anyway), *What shall I do?* With absolutely no effort or direction that I was conscious of, my hand made more letters on the page. I recognized them as I made them: *Write.* I thought, "What shall I write?" My hand wrote, *You'll know.* I wondered, *Can I come to you again?* More letters appeared: *Yes.*

The robe sank to the floor again, and I was in the doorway watching it. The scene disappeared, and though I recreated it, nothing happened in it without my intentionally deciding it should happen. The visitation was over.

The "revealed" words that I had written seem almost meaningless when printed on this page outside the historical and emotional context in which the event took place; but in my feeling about the memory, they were linked with the presence of the angel. What I got out of the experience was an awareness of my inner resources and my spiritual purposes. In fact, I have never since doubted my direction or purpose so strongly that a recollection of the basement/tower with its monk/angel has not brought some degree of renewed clarity and energy for work.

Reflection on these experiences raises another set of questions. How do I know that the light and the monk were angels, and not merely creations of my imagination? Furthermore, if these really were spiritual influences from outside myself, how do I know that they were good influences—angelic, not demonic? These things cannot be determined scientifically, or proved logically, although my internal certainty that they were angelic is virtually complete. Beyond that, these questions will be dealt with to some extent as we proceed in our discussion.

Angels Help People Celebrate

When people receive good news, resolve a problem, win a prize, or have any other reason to celebrate, one of their first impulses is to tell someone. Joy by its nature is more delightful when it is shared, and celebration works best as a corporate activity. Since people always are near spirits and angels who share their values, goals, and attitudes, they have a congenial audience ready at all times to share their joys and celebrations. This is as true for bad people, accompanied by evil spirits, as it is for good people who enjoy the companionship of good spirits and angels.

Some people may be accustomed already to thinking of this in religious contexts. When celebrating God's mercy with songs of praise and in prayer, it is not uncommon to think of angels sharing in this activity and to find the celebration enhanced by this feeling of angelic participation in worship.

This does happen, in fact, perhaps more often than people realize. Angels who particularly enjoy praising God are angels who especially like to sing. Therefore, when we really feel the joy of a song of praise that we are singing, we are unusually close to those angels, and sometimes we feel some of the joy that radiates from them.

But this kind of celebration with the angels, and the great joy that accompanies it, occurs in many situations other than in worship. Whenever you are doing something useful—whether a favor for a neighbor, a cooperative task with a friend, or a routine daily job—and find yourself enjoying what you are doing, part of that joy comes to you from nearby angels. Angels particularly enjoy doing things that benefit someone; and when you are enjoying your task for its own sake—simply taking pleasure in doing it well and knowing that it is helpful or valuable to someone—you put yourself in angelic company and share some of their heavenly happiness.

This shared happiness is less obvious in human experience than it is for angels. Angels feel the joy of being useful as vividly as humans feel the warmth of the sun on a spring day, but humans experience it primarily in the spiritual levels of the mind, which are subconscious most of the time, as will be shown later. The result is a kind of inner glow, a sense of well being. As indistinct as such joy is to the physical senses, it is a major component of the satisfaction that comes from living a useful life, and it is a heavenly gift, coming to us from the angels around us.

Celebrations of this kind occur during recreation, too. Part of the enjoyment that athletes, musicians, and others find in repeated practice (without which practice would be unbearably dull), comes from sharing the joy of nearby spirits who are celebrating the accomplishment of doing something well. Some of the pleasure afforded by concerts, recitals, and other musical events stems from the companionship of spirits who are attracted to the person who is deep in spiritual enjoyment. This is especially likely to occur while listening to music, because music affects the spirit more directly than other kinds of communication.

The reasons that this is true offer a glimpse into the relationship between the angels' spiritual environment and our physical world. The two realities are connected by a pervasive system called correspondence, which will be discussed in more detail, especially in chapter 3. One aspect of that system is that everything in this world, everything our physical senses perceive, reflects something in the spiritual realm that can be seen, heard, touched, smelled by angels and other spirits.*

Spirits around us participate in our activities especially when our "action" is almost exclusively mental and emotional. When we concentrate to such an extent that physical activity is limited—when even breathing, pulse, and

---

*According to Swedenborg, this connection explains the individual characteristics of physical things, such as musical sounds. Singing expresses feelings, and vocalized vowels (without words) convey pure feeling more vividly and sensitively than even the most evocative poetry. Stringed instruments, which originally were developed to emulate the human voice, have a similar effect. Distinguishable from the feelings themselves, this expression of feelings is the peculiar genius of the singing voice and its instrumental imitators because it originates in the lungs, and the lungs in the body reflect the spiritual ability to recognize and express what is true.

Trumpets, flutes or pipes evoke feelings more effectively than they express them. This distinction is more subtle in physical instruments than the spiritual difference it represents. Angels hear voices and stringed instruments in association with feelings about ideas, and trumpets in connection with what they love. The interplay between trumpet and chorus in the "Hallelujah Chorus" from Handel's *Messiah* illustrates the distinction.

blood pressure are diminished—the clarity of our spiritual connections increases. Although we generally are as invisible to the sight of spirits as spirits are to our physical vision, concentration that is deep enough—sufficiently self-absorbing—sometimes makes us visible to the spirits around us. When this happens, their influence on our thoughts and feelings is much stronger and more perceptible than in the normal course of our subconscious interaction.

At all times, we are surrounded by spirits or angels who share our goals and values, whether or not we are conscious of them or they of us; so whether we work or play, grieve or rejoice, it is normal for our spiritual companions to interact with our thoughts and feelings. If we learn to recognize their influence, we will find some of our feelings intensified and others modified. We will receive suggestions to help us interpret our perceptions, impulses toward actions we have not considered before, and ideas we have never thought of. These feelings and thoughts always come to us in ways that allow us to ignore them, or to take credit for them as our own. Cultivating a recognition of their source and their character, however, significantly increases our ability to deal with the issues of our lives.

2. Angels and Spirits

Several references in the previous chapter to "angels and spirits," or "angels and other spirits," imply a distinction between the two terms. *Spirit* or *spirits*, without modification, are the most general terms for all people who have lived and died, and live now only in the spiritual world. Angels are good spirits, living in heaven. Evil spirits are called just that, most of the time, though occasionally they are called "spirits from hell," since that is where they live, or "devils."

There also are spirits who are not in heaven or hell, that is, not angels or devils, but spirits who are still working on the transition from their life in a physical body to their life in a totally spiritual body and environment. These spirits—the "others," in "angels and other spirits"—live in a "world of spirits," intermediate between heaven and hell. This world of spirits is where spirits are still in the process of getting to know themselves, sorting out the apparent qualities that they had developed during their physical life, working through to the absolutely honest reality of themselves that is transparently obvious to the angels.

These spirits still feel some of their former attachment to physical and worldly things, so they are more like us (human spirits still living a physical life) than angels are. Therefore, they can relate to us and communicate with us more easily and more naturally than angels. In fact, we (human spirits still enveloped in a physical body) are always in the company of spirits from the world of spirits—spirits whose purposes and values are most like ours at any given time—and they are the ones with whom we have the most frequent and commonplace spiritual contact. This is the reason that most good spiritual influences come to us through spirits from angels.

Contact with spirits is unconscious—or subconscious—most of the time, for most of us. Indeed, many times we cannot tell whether our good ideas or guiding principles come from our own imagination and good judgment or from spiritual inspiration or leading. For example, if you had an Aunt Josephine who often reminded you while she lived that honesty is the best policy, and you think of her advice as you speak the truth under circumstances when it is difficult to do so, is that your memory and conscience, or immediate spiritual influence from Aunt Josephine's spirit? It could be either, or both reinforcing each other.

Sometimes, however, when the matter is urgent, with significant spiritual consequences for our life, conscious communication of some sort becomes necessary. Perhaps through vividly remembered dreams or visions seen in a hypnagogic state; occasionally by a "sign" that jolts us out of continuing on our unthinking course in a wrong direction; sometimes through "daydreamt" visions; and sometimes simply interrupting whatever we are doing or thinking about; in some way that is best for us at the time, spirits are seen, or heard, or both. All of these kinds of contact can be dismissed, or explained away as something else, with relative ease if someone wants to do that. That is why I am convinced that conscious spiritual contact occurs more often, with more people, than most of us realize. Even so, such contact with spirits is rare in our time and culture, at least in comparison to subconscious spiritual influences. Direct communication from angels is even more rare.

Furthermore, spirits are so much like us that they seem, sound, or appear familiar. Spirits of loved ones, who under special circumstances sometimes appear briefly just after they die, look just as they did before they died. Angels, on the other hand, are radically unfamiliar. Although they look to each other like the human beings they once were, they often appear in the world of spirits as images the spirits can recognize (perhaps as light too bright to look at directly, or some other representation of themselves). While angels do have the power to appear to spirits, or even to physical men or women, as a person or as anything that would serve their purpose, this seldom happens. Most of the time, angels that people see appear as someone (or something) the person has never seen before.

The angels or cherubim who guarded Eden were accompanied by a flaming sword that moved on its own (Gen. 3:24), and the angel who wrestled with Jacob (Gen. 32:24) looked like a man whom Jacob did not know. The angel who destroyed five thousand Assyrians (Isa. 37:36) was unseen, at least by the living, but the angels or seraphim that Isaiah saw in the temple (Isa. 6:2) and the "living creatures" that Ezekiel saw by the river Chebar (Ezek. 1:4-28) were unlike any man or beast seen by physical eyes. Isaiah's cherubim "each had six wings; with two he covered his face, and with two he covered his feet, and with two he did fly." Ezekiel's vision was even more surreal, each living creature having the face of a human, a lion, an ox, and an eagle, riding a chariot of wheels within wheels bearing a sapphire throne with a human figure of flame and amber.

As contemporary examples, consider the appearance of the angel in my dream and in my dreamlike experience in the basement/tower. The light, which I felt had personality and purpose, fits what I would expect an angel to look like to my eyes, and it had the power that I associate with angels. The robed "monk" also seems angelic to me, partly because of the improbability of the basement/tower scene and because the figure itself never appeared to me (I saw only the robe). I cannot say with certainty that they were not spirits with an appearance I took for angelic, but I believe they were angels.

The accuracy of my analysis is beside the point here, of course. Angels and spirits are distinguishable in the spiritual world, however uncertain our perceptions of them may be.

Evil Spirits

Another reason for thinking separately about angels and spirits is that only good spirits are angels; but not all spirits are good. In some cases, the process of self-recognition that spirits go through after physical death results in the spirit feeling most comfortable among evil companions. In other words, when spirits come to full self-understanding, they may find themselves at home in hell. The reason someone would choose hell will be explained later. Such spirits—those

Evil spirits chose false goals over true ones.

from hell and those in the world of spirits who are tending in that direction—are just as capable of influencing our lives, even of communicating with us by conscious contact, as good spirits and angels are.

That may be an alarming thought, but there are some qualifications to it. First of all, the spirits most closely associated with our human spirits at any particular time are those whose goals and motives are most similar to ours. That means that when we are doing something that is good and useful to others and concentrating fully on what we are doing, two good things follow: evil spirits stay away from us because they do not share that kind of purpose and value; and the good spirits who are attracted to us help keep evil spirits away.

Secondly, God and all the angels of heaven will help to protect us from evil influences, so long as that is what we really want. Angels and spirits will help us avoid or resist evil whenever their help is what we want most, but they will never force their aid upon us.

Neither of these kinds of protection, however, guards us completely against evil influences that we find appealing enough to consider. When we contemplate doing something selfish or engage in that kind of activity, we invite the companionship of selfish spirits. When we devise a scheme that benefits us at others' expense, we join the community of devious and self-seeking spirits. Spiritual help is available for any purpose we wholeheartedly intend—angels' help in achieving good goals or help from hell in accomplishing bad ones.

The same kinds of help are there for us when we are deciding between alternative actions. While we are really uncertain, both good and evil spirits are near us, each trying to influence the decision, each supplying us with reasons to support it or justify it. When we make up our mind as to what to do, one side draws even closer to us, pushing the other farther away. However, if we come to desire the outcome of one course of action, especially if we desire it for its own sake, without regard for what others might think of us for doing it, then spiritual support for the alternative recedes far into the background. In gaining spiritual companionship and support, our long-term intentions and basic values count for far more than one-time *ad hoc* decisions. It should be understood that even our best intentions are not unmixed with evil, and vice versa; but our better intentions seem polarized from our worse ones, and our choices appear to be between black and white.

A few years ago, much was made of a statement in a magazine article by then-President Jimmy Carter, to the effect that he had committed adultery in his heart (referring to Matt. 5:28). His comment raised for many (who perhaps had thought less about the Gospel than about adultery) a question of the possibility of guilt or condemnation on the basis of an action that is considered but rejected or at least not carried out. In the context of our interaction with spirits, the issue becomes somewhat clearer.

A course of action, such as adultery, cannot be adopted or rejected without coming into conscious consideration, so there can be no virtue or guilt until that point. However, that is precisely the point at which both good and evil spirits draw near to the human spirit with conflicting influences. A man's decision not to seduce a married woman would seem to be a victory for the angels (and the person making the decision might feel it to be so). In the world of spirits, however, the decision would appear less important than the reasons for which it was made.

If the decision was made by a husband because adultery is a sin, that would be a victory for the angels. However, even if the choice were made on a less specific basis, the results could be an angelic triumph. He might have rejected the temptation simply because adultery "didn't seem right," or because it would violate his marriage vows. He might have based his decision on the damage adultery would cause to the marriage or the good conscience of the woman he "looked upon," or because she did not desire it. A decision against sexual relations for these or any other principles derived from respect for marriage, for personal commitments, or for another person would still be a greater or a lesser angelic victory, depending on the depth and universality of the principle involved.

On the other hand, if the husband decided not to commit adultery because he had a good reputation in the community and feared losing it if his act were to be discovered, his angelic companions would have had no reason to rejoice. Similarly, if he avoided the behavior because he was afraid of the woman's husband, or was protecting himself in some other way, or simply because no suitable opportunity appeared available to him, then victory (greater or lesser depending on the reasons involved) would belong to the spirits from hell. If he intended to commit adultery but was restrained only by fear of some danger to himself, then adulterous spirits would have a stronger connection with him than they did before, as would self-serving spirits who place a higher value on reputation, personal safety, and the like, than on higher principles. Furthermore, these connections would increase the difficulty that good spirits might have in influencing his future decisions.

This ability of evil spirits to attach themselves to our intentions when those intentions are evil—or merely not good—raises important danger signals for people who are considering seeking open communication with spirits. Blanket encouragement or condemnation of such practices misses the point. What is crucial is our most fundamental motivation in seeking contact with a spirit. This deepest motive, our spiritual intention, may well be subconsciously guiding our rational explanation or justification and what it is is most relevant to the spirits around us.

Our choice of spiritual companionship is not the only element affecting our lives under God's purposes and loving kindness, but it is a significant factor. If, in the spirit of wholehearted love of God that motivates acts of love and service toward the people around you, you seek heavenly guidance in completing some useful task, that intention will attract angels and other spirits who would be truly helpful. But if you seek contact with spirits out of adventurous curiosity, you attract adventurous spirits with an affinity for such curiosity—perhaps the kind who once wrote for the tabloids sold at supermarkets! Seeking contact to get an advantage in the stock market or at the pari-mutuel window (where spirits should have an advantage, being able to see our future from their perspective outside of time) would tend to attract "insider" traders or race "fixers." As a friend of mine put it, "If you wouldn't invest in a stock that Uncle Louie recommended when he was alive, what makes you think he's more honest now that he's dead?"

Of course, there are dangers in opening ourselves to increased spiritual influence that are too serious to make light of and that need not be explored here. Spirits and spiritual influences on our lives are real and powerful. Since our deepest, often unconscious, motivations have a lot to do with the spirits who are around, seeking contact is not a game to be played nor an activity to be taken lightly.

Yahweh's warning to Isaiah against seeking "them that have familiar spirits, and . . . wizards that peep and mutter" (Isa. 8:19) may seem irrelevant to modern, well-educated "sensitives," but the alternative to seeking out spirits remains an important choice. "Should not a people rather seek their God?", Isaiah wrote (Isa. 8:19), and this raises again the question of motive. Approaching a medium or sensitive as an alternative to prayer can be turning away from God. On the other hand, communication can be experienced from within an attitude of prayer. I know of a woman who, after praying for release from grief over the loss of her son, was sent by her minister to a well-known sensitive and found the comfort that she sought.

The Battleground

The image of good spirits and bad spirits, gathered with conflicting influences around a human spirit who is making some kind of a choice—something we humans do, quite a lot of the time—suggests another metaphor. A cliche, popular with political commentators, refers to the president's or Congress' or some political group's waging "a battle for the hearts and minds" of voters. The two kinds of spirits, those governed by heaven and those governed by hell, do indeed do battle for the hearts and minds of human spirits. Because we are spirits clothed in physical bodies, our lives are the battleground.

The apostle Paul wrote that "our struggle is not against enemies of blood and flesh, but against . . . spiritual forces of evil" (Eph. 5:10-17). From that perspective, it could be said that this battle is what life is all about. Our human bodies impel us from the start toward self-preservation, urging us strongly to seek food, clothing, and shelter—whatever we need to stay alive, healthy, and comfortable—without regard for others. Physical survival is self-centered, and this aspect of it can be exploited by evil spirits and turned into selfishness or (given the opportunity) tyranny. As we mature, our human spirit develops other values, loving certain other people, prizing certain things that do not contribute directly to our physical survival, and developing altruistic goals. These are qualities that good spirits encourage and develop into heavenly virtues.

Our physical existence and our spiritual life form what might be called our two human natures. Physical human nature includes our individual bodies and their innumerable and inextricable connections with other people and things in the material environment. This whole complex system, in turn, is intermeshed with our spiritual nature. For every individual, the bond between the two natures dissolves in physical death; but as long as our spirit lives in our body, the two natures remain systematically interdependent yet in tension or conflict with each other. The contrariety between these two natures in each of us, combined with our ability freely to choose which aspect of our selves to favor in each of life's multitude of decisions, is what shapes our personality and character. The kind of spirit that we really are, the true self that we discover during our stay in the world of spirits, is to a large extent the net result of all those decisions.

We human beings, who are spirits having physical bodies, are distinct from angels and other spirits, who are spirits having spiritual bodies. Our physical body's visible expression of invisible thoughts and feelings makes possible a second distinction between us and spirits—namely, our human ability to misrepresent our true feelings and intention. As Shakespeare's Hamlet put it, "One may smile and smile and be a villain." This is not entirely bad. The ability to dissemble may be necessary for survival. Much that we call "civilized" behavior involves smiling politely at competitors, opponents, even enemies in certain situations, and discussing with calm detachment things about which we care passionately. What parents call "serious talks" with their children provide one example. Peace conferences provide another: they could not begin if the individual participants could not hide their personal feelings to some extent. Deception is one of the weapons that may be in use at any time in the battleground of the physical world, in which spiritual qualities are developed. But in the spiritual world, where there are neither wars nor peace conferences and where there are no physical faces to misrepresent feelings, everyone's genuine feelings are transparent to all. This complete inability to dissemble makes it impossible for spirits to be comfortable among others with different values and purposes and prevents deception totally.

Being without the tension of our physical/spiritual makeup and without our ability to deceive, spirits find themselves with far fewer opportunities to be tempted. This means that they have fewer opportunities to make the kinds of decisions that form character. The principal opportunities for spiritual growth and development, therefore, lie in the life we are living now. The decisions we make, with or against the angels and angelic spirits around us, largely determine our ultimate place in the spiritual world—in heaven or in hell.

This is the circumstance that makes a knowledge of angels and spirits so valuable to us. When we are being tempted, when influences of evil spirits seem attractive or even compelling, some understanding of angels and spirits can help us in a couple of different ways.

For one thing, it can be helpful to know that the attractiveness of something, or the apparent compulsion toward a particular action, can rise out of the influence of evil spirits, rather than out of anything essential or unchangeable in ourselves or in the object of our desire. This knowledge can be power if we use it to objectify our feelings and our rationalizing thoughts, recognizing them as intruders to be repelled. Also, certainty that angels will repel the invading influences for us, if we wholeheartedly seek their help, can free us from the helpless feeling that we must inevitably succumb to the temptation.

Knowing about angels and spirits cannot help us, any more than the angels themselves can, if we really want to do what we are tempted to do. Angels can help only those who want help more than anything else, "who are forever striving," as Goethe's angels said about Faust. But if relief from the temptation is what we really want, relief is really there. Really. And it is an invincible relief.

Invincibility is one of the important characteristics of angels. Since they work, or fight, for what is true and good, the power of God—all the power there is—is available to them. No power from hell is equal to that of an angel, and entire hosts of angels can be summoned by prayer. The good and the true must inevitably triumph if they are called.

The living experience of temptation by evil spirits never feels as simple as it really is. For one thing, the truth behind the great one-liner "I can resist anything but temptation!" is that when we are seriously tempted it is not so easy to want the temptation removed. For another, our earthbound awareness may not perceive all the help we have received. In this case, when we pray for help and do not feel immediate and complete relief from the temptation, it is easy for evil spirits to convince us that our prayers have not been heard at all. If we give up then, when the angels have almost won, the devils' victory is all the more tragic. However, these dangers arise from our weaknesses, not the angels'. Although angels will not help us if we do not ask without reservation, they will conquer temptation if we do ask.

Few people really believe the popular but silly excuse for wrongdoing, "The Devil made me do it!" mostly because so few people believe in the Devil. But the reality of evil spirits, or devils, still gives no credibility to the old excuse, because although devils, or demonic powers, are fearfully real, none can stand before the power of a single angel, an angel who stands always ready if called. Whatever we do, no devil could have made us do it, unless at some level we *wanted* to do it. If we had unreservedly asked for help, we could have resisted the temptation with help from heaven.

Our experience of the struggle against temptation never appears to be this clearcut. Many people have discovered that their own Achilles' heel is in the ability to rationalize. As soon as we start to consider a choice between good and bad actions, or right and wrong motives, we begin to see the infinite shades of gray that really do exist between them and to wonder what we really want, or hope, or believe. Even if we do not begin to ask ourselves these questions, evil spirits always are ready to point them out. The positive side of this bleak picture lies in the help available from spirits and angels. When we quit trying to figure out for ourselves what is right or wrong, good or bad, but genuinely ask for help (being willing to accept it when it comes), the way becomes clear—at least clear enough for us to proceed. The darkness has not overcome the light (John 1:5) and the *devil* cannot *make* you do it.

The "Devil" who tempted Jesus, (Matt. 4) "Satan," (Luke 10:18), "the devil and his angels" (Matt. 25:41) refer either to one example or the totality of demonic power. They do not refer to a prince of evil who might in any sense be considered an equal opponent of God or a "creator of evil." In the ringing words of the prophet Isaiah, "I am Yahweh, and there is no other. I form light and create darkness, I make weal and create woe; I, Yahweh, do all these things" (Isa. 45:6-7). God's power, available to us directly or through angels, is all the power there is. But a portion of that power was given us by God in the divine act of creating us "a little lower than God" (Ps. 8:5): God gave us the power to choose whether we would accept his aid or not. Accounts of demonic possession of human minds, from the Gospel's healing narratives to the work of Paul Tillich, Rollo May, and M. Scott Peck, are vivid descriptions of terrifying reality. But I have found no depiction of the power of evil that weakens my confidence in the greater power of God and God's angels.

If you take seriously the image of life as a battlefield, you will want to be on the side of the angels!

Spirits Becoming Angels

Earlier in this chapter, spirits were described as working on their transition from physical life to purely spiritual life. In order to make that transition, they must accept the fact that, though they have "died," they still are alive. They also must become aware of their spiritual body, grow acquainted with the qualities of their spiritual environment, and gradually come to recognize their true character.

This last, the process of getting to know one's self, is the most difficult part for most people, and is by far the most important aspect of the transition. The characteristically human ability to mask true feelings and intentions with apparent ones is so effective that most of us manage to fool ourselves as well as others. If we try to figure out for ourselves what we really value most highly, or what we really would want most to do if all things were possible, or if no one could find out, the answer may come with difficulty, if at all. Furthermore, our answer may well change several times if we contemplate the question long enough.

Spirits do not have the same ability to deceive other spirits; but during the transition period, they are allowed a little time in which to realize that fact. Most spirits are allowed to work through their own self-deceptions, coming to self-awareness of their true nature, before they realize how they are seen by others. Some spirits achieve this realization quickly, having been radically honest with themselves in their introspection in human life. Others, who believed more deeply in the appearance or "front" that they presented to other people, need both time and help in getting to know themselves.

Newly arrived spirits join groups with similar values.

One experiential avenue to spirits' knowledge of themselves arises from the freedom and openness of spiritual life. Spirits need only turn their attention to a particular thing that they especially prize to find themselves immediately in the company of others who desire the same thing. Alternatively, beginning to plan some particularly enjoyable action places them among other spirits getting ready to do something similar. Thus, newly arrived spirits can enter groups of spirits with like values and intentions and quickly learn from experience whether they are comfortable among those spirits or not. If one spirit does not enjoy being with spirits who are planning to do what he always said (to himself and to others) he wanted to do, he soon is faced with the realization that he really wanted to do something else. If another spirit who always claimed a particular fondness for something feels out of place among others who love doing the same thing, she recognizes that her professed enthusiasm for the activity was only apparent and she really valued something else much more.

Since there may be many layers to our self-deception, some spirits must visit many spiritual communities before finding themselves at home—which is the same as finding their true selves. Spirits who feel most comfortably at home among others who prize what is true and intend what is good find themselves in heaven; and spirits who are at home in heaven are angels. There are countless communities in all levels of heaven, so every angelic spirit can find a true home.

Other spirits cannot be comfortable in any heavenly society, any more than a fish can live out of water. These find themselves most at home among hellish spirits who prize what is false and love to do harm to others. No externally imposed judgment is necessary to "send" them to hell. The absolute self-awareness of the spiritual world sorts spirits out so accurately that they find their home for themselves.

Because the self-assessment takes so long for many spirits, the world of spirits between heaven and hell is a busy place, filled with communities of spirits who still carry human memories and concerns. These are the spirits with whom people have most in common, the entities most easily reached through mediums, meditative techniques, or other ways of seeking direct contact. The fact that these spirits still are concerned with things that mattered to them while they lived in their body raises another warning about deliberately seeking contact with them. Their involvement with worldly and bodily matters causes much of their communication to be trivial or banal: elevating such advice because it comes from a spiritual source can lead to fixation or at least foolishness. In most cases, spirits themselves do not seek contact with people in this world, except under the direction of angels or, when we are inclined to welcome such spirits, the supervision of devils.

3. Who Says So?

Most of what has been said about angels to this point—insights not drawn from my experience or that of friends—comes from Emanuel Swedenborg. He was an eighteenth-century mining engineer and theoretical scientist who tells of having spent the last twenty-seven years of his life in almost daily conversation with angels and other spirits. Of course, the nature of the case precludes our knowing anything about his experience outside of what he reported. Thus, it is essential to ask what kind of a reporter Swedenborg was.*

The Man

Descended on both sides of his family from operators and owners of Sweden's mines and smelters, Emanuel Swedenborg (1688-1772) was the son of a preacher who became dean of the Theology Department at Uppsala University and

---

*The following paragraphs offer biographical information that bears directly on the issue of Swedenborg's credibility. Readers who want more information may wish to consult George F. Dole and Robert H. Kirven, *A Scientist Explores Spirit: A Compact Biography of Emuanuel Swedenborg with Key Concepts of Swedenborg's Theology* (New York City and West Chester, PA: Swedenborg Foundation, 1992). It contains additional information about Swedenborg's life, a bibliographic guide to other biographies and source materials, and a summary of his key theological ideas.

Emanuel Swedenborg (1688–1772)

eventually Bishop of Skara. Young Swedenborg had the benefit of an excellent tutor, an Uppsala education, years of study with mathematicians in England and France, and an apprenticeship to Sweden's leading inventor, all by the time he was thirty. By age thirty-six, he had inherited a modest income for life, was a member of the board in charge of Sweden's mining industry, a member of the House of Nobles in the Swedish parliament, a friend of the country's political elite, and was regularly welcomed at the royal court. His mining duties and interests led him into theoretical mineralogy; and by age forty-six, he had published a three-volume Latin work on the subject, known in English as *Philosophical and Mineralogical Works*. This was widely acclaimed throughout Europe, and parts of it were translated into several languages.

Next, he began a scientific search for the soul. This was a popular intellectual quest during the heyday of the British and European Enlightenment, engaging such minds as Descartes, Leibniz, Newton, and Rousseau, among others. Swedenborg's approach was characteristic of his scientific and practical approach to life: considering the soul as cause or active agent and the physical body as its effect or area of action, he decided to search for the soul by analyzing the physical body. He based his analysis on the still-developing technology of human dissection. He had observed some of the leading dissectionists during his travels and had gained some experience in the field, so he considered doing his own dissections for his new project. But he abandoned that approach, relying instead on published works, for the explicit reason that he found it harder to be objective about his own discoveries than about those of others, and he wanted his search for the soul to be carefully scientific. He was proof-reading galleys for the third volume of a work on the soul, which he had projected to eight volumes, when suddenly his work was interrupted by a series of remarkable psychic events.

Before these events are described, however, we should emphasize what a practical man Swedenborg was. When in his early twenties, he designed "a machine to fly in the air," for which he computed the area-to-weight ratio necessary for a fixed-wing craft, provided a landing gear and a cockpit for a pilot—and allowed there might be a few broken bones if the design were ever implemented. These are firsts in the history of aircraft design, but more importantly, they demonstrate a realistic and practical mind. Although he engineered many technological advances that enhanced the economics of mining and smelting, his first inventions in this area were devices to ease the labor and reduce the danger of mining. His mineralogical works were milestones in the development of that science.

Moreover, the physiological analyses he performed in his search for the soul soundly anticipated acknowledged breakthroughs in the science of human reproduction by half a century. Also, he correctly identified the function of the cerebral cortex and its pyramid cells more than a hundred years before these were recognized by the scientific community. A 1910 study by Martin Ramström, a professor at the University of Uppsala, showed that Swedenborg had indeed based his analytical speculations on a valid reading of published dissection results (rather than "fudging" the evidence), and had drawn conclusions from them that were truly original (not "borrowed" from the original authors). There is, in fact, every evidence that Swedenborg was a solid scientist, as well as a faithful and fiscally conservative member of Sweden's parliament.

Still, Swedenborg was not immune to non-scientific influences. While he was working on his physiological search for the soul, he closely observed his mental and emotional processes. He noticed that when he breathed only minimally—that is, he hypoventilated—he was able to concentrate more productively. Practicing this hypoventilated thinking, he began to notice a "cheering light," and "a little blue flame" in his mind's eye, the flame appearing when he was on the right track or approaching a valid conclusion.

Also, while publishing the first volumes of his work on the soul, he began experiencing unusual mood swings and periods of having strange dreams. Characteristically, he recorded all this in a journal, along with a record of what the dreams seemed to mean to him when he first awoke. In doing so, he was the first modern scientific writer to keep a record of his dreams. He appears to have been fully aware of psychic processes in his experience and to have treated them as rationally as he did the findings of dissectionists or any other data that he had at hand.

It is fair to say that Swedenborg was an accomplished and practical empiricist—aware of psychic developments within him, but solidly "in control" of himself as well. At the time, Swedenborg was approaching what was to be a dramatic juncture in his life.

One day during Holy Week of 1744, Swedenborg picked up galley proofs from his printer in The Hague. As was his custom, he traveled through nearby Dutch cities while he read them. After attending Easter services in Amsterdam, he traveled the next day to Delft. He continued recording unusual dreams and noted on Sunday night that he felt especially unworthy of God's loving grace. On Monday afternoon, however, he was seized with a feeling of bliss. Then, in the middle of the night, he woke to a violent trembling that threw him on the floor, where he found himself in the arms of the Lord Jesus Christ.

He felt himself charged by this visitation with a commission that he remembered as a Swedish phrase, *"Nå så giör,"* meaning roughly, "Do it!" but he recorded that he understood it to mean, "Do what you have promised." He spent several hours struggling with doubts: it would be a sin of pride to imagine himself visited by the Christ if it were only an illusion. But would it not be a worse sin to deny the presence of the Lord if it were true? Toward morning, he felt a sense of comfort, and eventually fell asleep, dreaming that his father, who had died a few years before, appeared to him with a sign of approval.

Waking on Tuesday morning, he recorded all this in his journal just as he recorded the dreams of other nights, except that he noted in the margin that this was a very important entry. He shows no awareness of any parallels between his experience and the "direct calling" of others in the devo-

tional tradition, including Zinzendorf and (later) Wesley.
About a year following the first visitation, after he had made
some uncertain attempts to do as he believed he had been
commanded, he received a more specific commission to pub-
lish for the world the inner meaning found in the Bible, a
spiritual sense within the literal text.

From that night in 1745, until his death in 1772, he had
almost daily experiences of visiting heaven, hell, and the intermediate "state" he called "the world of spirits." He traveled through all these, conversed with angels and good and
evil spirits whom he met there, and was given living demon-
strations in his mind and body of various kinds of angelic
and spiritual influences.

This continuing series of spiritual encounters provided
fundamental data for his theological writings during those
twenty-seven years, constituting thirty volumes in the stan-
dard English edition. Information about angels and other
spirits can be found throughout that body of work, but several sections within it are especially rich in this material.

One is a series of articles published between early chapters of his first and largest theological work, *Arcana Coelestia*, originally published in eight Latin volumes between
1749 and 1756. This "inter-chapter material" is located between paragraphs 67 and 2893 (Swedenborg numbered all
his paragraphs, so these references are uniform in all edi-
tions). A second resource is the entire contents of what probably is Swedenborg's all-time best seller, *Heaven and Hell*,
first published in 1758. The third is a series of accounts of
spiritual experiences reported between the chapters of three

of his works, *Apocalypse Revealed*, first published in 1766, *Conjugial Love* (1768), and *True Christian Religion* (1771), which stories are found under the heading of "Memorabilia" in some translations and "Memorable Relations" or just "Relations" in others.

The Message

Several themes are prominent in what Swedenborg wrote about angels. It should be understood, however, that in his theological writing, considered as a whole, Swedenborg's primary message is not focused specifically on angels. He was much more concerned with the importance of loving God, serving one's neighbor, and pursuing personal spiritual growth. Swedenborg himself once wrote that if there is such a thing as Swedenborgianism, it would be the worship of the Lord Jesus Christ. One of his biographers, Ernst Benz, wrote that Swedenborg's basic message was "the same as the earliest form of the Gospel, 'Repent! for the Kingdom of Heaven is at hand.'"

However it is phrased, the central focus of Swedenborg's religious writings is an effort to communicate his revelation with the intent of changing his reader's beliefs and way of life, with salvation as the goal. Swedenborg conveys much of the substance of this message in accounts of angels and spirits whom he met and about whom he had a lot to say.

Probably Swedenborg's most important teaching about angels is that they are not special creations apart from human life. Angels and other spirits once were human beings

Since angels were once human, they have an affinity with us.

living the life that all of us know on this earth or another in the universe. Those whom we are most likely to encounter lived on this earth recently—within our lifetime—and within the culture we are most familiar with. Most if not all biblical occurrences of the word "angel" describe a messenger from God, and it is tradition, not biblical authority, that describes them as special creations.

Closely related to Swedenborg's assertion that all angels come from human life is his principle that we ourselves really are spirits, even while we live in our bodies. In Heaven and Hell (433), he states the following:

> Since everything that is alive in the body belongs strictly to the spirit (also everything that acts and senses as a result of life), none of it belonging to the body, it follows that the spirit is the actual person.

From his experience in the spiritual world, Swedenborg learned that this fact of our essential spiritual nature makes it theoretically possible for us to converse with the angels and spirits who are around us and to share their experiences. In fact, he says that this was common at the dawn of human history. It no longer happens in the normal course of events because the human race has developed such a dominant tendency to care more about physical and worldly concerns than about spiritual ones. When this attitude is reversed, however, individuals can become as aware of the presence of spirits and angels as they are of their physical companions.

Not only were spirits and angels once human beings, but they continue to look, sound, and feel like humans to themselves and to other spirits. In Swedenborg's time, at least—and there is not much reason to suppose things have changed greatly in this respect—spirits who had recently died were surprised to find that their appearance, their surroundings, and their inner feelings were much the same as before they died. Some, of course, were surprised to find themselves in any condition, having been convinced that they would not exist at all after they had died. Beside these, however, most of those who had expected some kind of life after death were surprised to find themselves with their human appearance—surprised especially that they, like those around them, and the gardens, houses, or whatever surroundings they saw, were so real, so unexpectedly solid and substantial. Some expected to find themselves wispy, somehow vague, or ethereal. Although Swedenborg does not mention it, many of them—influenced then as we are today by depictions of angels in medieval and modern art—were surprised to find themselves without wings, halos, white robes and standard-issue harps. The self-selecting process that takes the place of the widely anticipated "Judgment" must have surprised many, as well.

Swedenborg reported that angels and spirits have all the senses that humans have, raised to a much higher degree of sensitivity and they register on all five senses as being completely real and substantial. Indeed, spirits who have died suddenly, without any mental preparation for their transition, may find themselves at first in circumstances so much like those of their physical life that it takes some time (what might seem to us as days or months, depending on their ability to adapt mentally) and sometimes some persuasion, for them to come to believe that they actually have died. People who did not believe in life after death have a similar difficulty in accepting their demise.

Swedenborg met one such spirit. He was both amazed, and apparently a little amused, at the unusual firmness of the spirit's conviction that he was a physical person in the physical world, having no idea what a soul might be. In an effort to convince him of the reality of his situation, Swedenborg pointed out that the spirit was not standing on the ground, but in the air a little above Swedenborg's head. Drawing attention to this discrepancy apparently convinced the skeptic, because Swedenborg tells how he "ran off" in terror, shouting, "I am a spirit! I am a spirit!"

Angels wear clothes, as people do on earth, each having a variety of garments from which to choose for different days and occasions. Their clothing is not for warmth or for protection from anything like the inconvenient elements of our physical atmosphere. Rather, angels' garments project something about the truths that they embody and their understanding or acceptance of their truth.

Angels live in houses, located in communities in such a way that everyone's neighbors are those who share the same values and goals. Each angel's house relates—in its size, the beauty of its design, its furnishings, and its gardens—to the quality of good that the angel embodies.

They all have work to do, and periods of recreation, as well as other times for rest. Their whole heavenly world is a continuation of everything in our physical world that is related to true and eternal things. The relationship of clothes, houses, and so forth to true and eternal things is one in which the visible things represent the invisible ones in such a perfect and essential way that an angel's home, clothes, possessions, and occupation project the deepest and most significant aspects of the angel's character.

The inherent relationship between people and spirits makes our spiritual companions the natural medium for God to use in guiding, supporting, and assisting us in many ways. Their power to help us is almost unlimited, within boundaries that God has set. These restrictions preserve our human freedom of choice. Within those bounds, spiritual help is available to us for the asking. Angelic aid never is forced upon us, but always is there when we need and seek it.

As certain as he was about the power and accessibility of spiritual support, however, Swedenborg did not underestimate the difficulty of living on the battleground of life. To call upon angelic reinforcements is not as easy in practice as it may seem, because the angels' enemies have powerful means to keep us from seeking that help. For one thing, our instinct for self-preservation is not only a springboard to selfishness, as mentioned earlier; it also becomes a deterrent to our belief in the reality of help for our particular situation.

From childhood's schoolyard fights, through learning to drive defensively and to budget our resources, and countless other life experiences, we have learned to depend on our intelligence and strength to get through difficulties. Long after we have accepted the principle that God and the angelic host are on our side, we continue to fall back on our instinctive self-reliance when the going gets tough. The more successful we have been, the greater the pull toward self-sufficiency— and with it, the feeling of being alone and vulnerable. Worse yet, "assurances" of spiritual assistance at such a time may leave us open to feelings of guilt and self-condemnation, because we are still in the situation from which prayer is supposed to have rescued us.

The course to take in a difficult situation is, first of all, to respect the difficulty (sometimes even danger) the situation presents, and second, to adopt an attitude that Swedenborg calls "as if." This approach, developed more fully in the next chapter, is to work (or fight, or whatever the situation demands) as if we alone were responsible for dealing with the problem before us, but at the same time to pray for divine help, remembering that only God (directly or through angels) can make our ability sufficient to the challenge that we face.

Can You Believe It?

One way of answering this question is to present evidence that supports what Swedenborg says about angels in action. He was described earlier as an educated, capable, and responsible scientist, the kind of reporter who can be trusted— at least, trusted within reasonable bounds of probability. Claiming to have walked and talked with angels every day for twenty-seven years might strain those bounds for most people. However, there is more to be said about Swedenborg's trustworthiness.

There is the problem of slander. Some church leaders were upset by Swedenborg's writings. Some in Sweden—for example, a certain Bishop Lamberg and a Dean Ekebom— heard through the grapevine that his books were unorthodox, and (using the kind of logic that typifies political and religious witch hunts to this day) wanted to ban his books without reading them. Also, the Swedish Lutheran pastor in London, Aaron Mathesius, circulated a story impugning Swedenborg's sanity. The story was that at the height of a brilliant scientific career, Swedenborg fell ill with a high fever, was seen rolling naked in the gutter of the street, and *shortly after that* began writing about spirits and heretical theological notions. The story was circulated widely enough that John Wesley heard it and mentioned it in his journal as fact.

The slander was very disturbing to friends who knew that Swedenborg had been eminently sane and rational up to the time of his death. While eyewitnesses to his behavior were still alive and the memories fresh, his friends collected and published testimonials. Servants who waited on him, scholars who discussed theology with him, friends who entertained him at dinner, all went on the record as testifying to his completely normal and charming discourse and behavior. By numerous reliable and contemporary accounts, Swedenborg was as capable and consistent when he wrote about angels as when he accurately computed the area-to-weight lift factors for a workable aircraft.*

Another argument for Swedenborg's believability is the nature of the writings themselves. Despite the difficulties that nineteenth-century English translations present to modern readers, they were written in an elegantly simple Latin. This gives the impression of a writer trying to be clear, rather than persuasive. (In earlier works, Swedenborg had demonstrated his mastery of ornate oratorical Latin.) His works show virtually no attempt to convince the reader with anything other than the accumulation of coherent data.

An important feature of his work that has impressed several commentators is the massive system of referencing. His formulations of theological principles are corroborated by copious references to the Bible (true authority for a devout Swedish Lutheran) and by references to related passages he had written in earlier volumes. The number and frequency of these

---

*Over 200 pages of these testimonials are printed in R.L. Tafel, ed., *Documents Concerning Swedenborg*, two volumes bound as three (London: Swedenborg Society, 1875-1892). See vol. 2, part I, pp. 572-612.

references, as well as the internal coherence to which they testify, form in themselves an argument compelling to many.

These evidences of Swedenborg's credibility, to which others might be added, are convincing to some, but beside the point for others. The people who first collected or observed them were people who already had read what Swedenborg wrote, believed it, and were looking for objective arguments to support their belief. Skeptical readers may admit that such data make Swedenborg believable, but fall short of proving that what he said is true.

That is not surprising, given the nature of knowledge and belief. It has been noted frequently that Thomas Aquinas' proofs for the existence of God have never been disproven logically, but neither have they induced the conversion of a single person to belief in God. The inescapable lesson to be drawn from detailed observation of the process of coming to believe is that people will find reasons for believing what they want to believe—and they will not be convinced by any logical reasoning to believe anything against their will.

Still, we know that people do change their minds (aided, perhaps, by angels), and come to believe things that earlier they had doubted or denied. This often happens because people deeply long for what they know to hang together without contradiction, and this desire may overcome a reluctance to believe some particular thing when the evidence warrants. Reluctance can also be overcome when a new idea fits, as it were, in a space that had been blank in a person's conception of reality. This is as true in scientific practice as it is in theology.

Countless people have experienced one or both of these compulsions to believe when they read Swedenborg. One woman, who was quite elderly when I met her in my youth, told of a highly compressed form of the experience. About 1900, she had been studying osteopathy (she later became a D.O.), and her husband was preparing for ministry in the Episcopal Church. The husband later became a Swedenborgian minister. However, when he first told his wife of his intention to leave the Episcopal Church and study Swedenborg, they argued so violently that they stopped speaking to each other. One night, after they had eaten together in silence and were reading at the cleared dining table under the best light in the house, he quit reading and—without speaking—went to bed, leaving his book open.

The woman finished the chapter she was reading in her book and then, as she reached across the table to turn out the light, caught sight of a passage in her husband's book that attracted her to read a little more. The book was Swedenborg's *Heaven and Hell*. She read it to the end, then started back at the beginning, reading to the place she had started, and finished just in time to fix breakfast and announce to her husband that the silence and the argument were ended, for she was ready to become a Swedenborgian too.

She liked to relate how everything she read that momentous night impressed her as something she had suspected, or had hoped was true, but never had heard or read before. She had wanted to remain in the security and familiarity of the faith she had grown up with, but her desire to believe what she was reading was stronger.

The pull of an open book and the effect of a desire to believe have drawn people away from Swedenborg, as well as toward him. They once drew me away. Looking back from where I stand now, it does not seem that they led me astray so much as that they led me through a path to a better place—a place I might not have been able to reach in any other way. Both theory and experience convince me that angels stimulate that desire to believe, doing so at the right time, as considered from God's perspective rather than from our own.

People who want to believe what Swedenborg described about angels in action will find that they can and that clear enough reasons to support that belief will emerge.

4. What He Said

A particular understanding of people, of human nature, was mentioned in several earlier chapters. It begins with the conception that the living, thinking, feeling, loving, and acting aspects of a human being are spiritual. Being spiritual, each thinking and acting human person is immortal.

Human Nature

That conception is incomplete, however, without its necessary qualification that a human being living in the physical world is clothed with a physical body, which cannot be separated from its spirit except by death. Paranormal experiences, described as out-of-body, astral, and the like, involve extraordinary perception, projection, and other remarkable capabilities of the mind, rather than actual separation of the spirit from the body. A spirit without a body is not a human being but a spirit; a body without a spirit is not a human being but a corpse; a human being is a spirit interactively enveloped in a body.

This complex being, a spirit living in and acting through a body, is characterized by a tension between good and bad impulses, along with the consequent ability to change and grow, as was described in chapter 2. The spirit relates to the body through the body's senses, and yet the physical senses are dulled or sharpened, focused, and directed by the spirit.

So long as it lives in its body, the spirit's ability to achieve its goals remains totally dependent on the body. The spirit is conscious of its physical surroundings only through the body, and the body's brain can be aware of spiritual things only through the spirit.

The complex relationship between the two is partially illustrated by the diagram. The diagram is limited, of course, by its stationary nature, which conceals the dynamics of body-spirit interaction; but it does help in defining the relationships between components of consciousness.

All three of the overlapping circles represent aspects of the human spirit. If the body were shown in the diagram, it would be overlapping the lower circle, from one perspective, or completely surrounding the lower two and overlapping the third, from another. The areas of overlap indicate interfaces or areas of interaction between what might be called levels of human spiritual nature. That is not quite the right term, however: since each circle represents a necessary component of human nature, they cannot be ranked higher or lower in priority or importance. As Paul observed about parts of the body: "The body is one and has many members, and all the members of the body, though many, are one body" (1 Cor. 12:12-26).

The lower circle represents what might be called the neuroconsciousness, the spiritual interface with the body's neurological systems. It is the level of unconscious awareness of the body's sensory input, and the (also unconscious) control and coordination of muscles by which the mind's intentions are enacted. It is the aspect of the spiritual mind in which all sensory impressions are recorded, including far more data

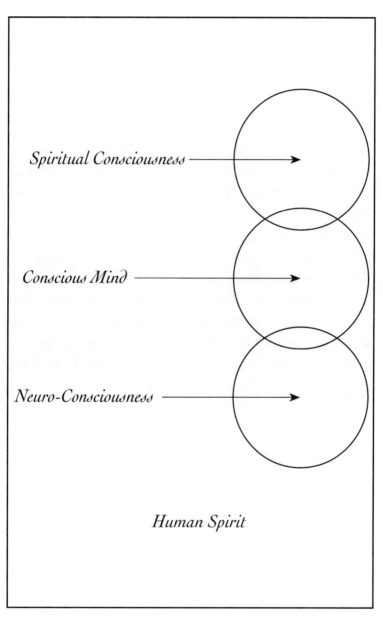

Aspects of the Human Spirit

than are normally selected for awareness in the conscious mind represented by the middle circle.

The top circle represents spiritual consciousness, including awareness of one's spiritual surroundings and companionship, and of all kinds of spiritual influence. Like the lower circle, this one is unconscious, aware of far more data from its environment than are admitted into the middle circle.

The center, then, is consciousness, or the conscious mind, which, because it thinks, feels, and intends, is spiritual. Consciousness overlaps the upper and lower circles, because whenever we are conscious, we are aware to some extent of both physical and spiritual influences. If the diagram were as dynamic as the reality it models, the areas of overlap would be continually increasing or diminishing, as we admit into conscious awareness more or less of the physical and spiritual inputs gathered from our two natural environments.

While we meditate, for example, the upper overlap expands nearly to fill the center circle; in other words, successful meditation crowds out almost all physical awareness—temperature, lights in the room, perhaps even the ringing of a telephone, may go unnoticed (i.e., the lower overlap is diminished), while we are more aware than usual of spiritual influences. At another extreme, when we are playing a quick-response video game, input from eyes, ears, and the touch of our fingertips on the control buttons dominates our mind and leaves us oblivious to spiritual goals, values, and other influences—as well as neural input regarding temperature, audible calls to dinner, or anything else that might detract from our game-focused skills.

Our physical life is only one layer of our existence.

Most of the time, our conscious mind controls how much input it receives from both our neuroconsciousness and our spiritual consciousness. Sometimes, however, one or another breaks in, making us aware of something, whether we want to recognize it or not. We may be concentrating almost all our attention on reading an exciting book, for instance, when steadily waning afternoon light finally reaches a level of dimness that forces awareness of the physical environment, and we turn on a light. Likewise, we may be focusing diligently on something physical, such as cleaning the house or working in the shop, when a spiritual commitment clamors for attention, and we realize that we must stop to attend to the needs of someone who depends on our care. Occasionally, in more dramatic circumstances, spiritual influence breaks into our consciousness as an inner voice that we feel we have heard (as if it were physical), or even as an apparition. Although such intrusions are relatively rare, they do occur frequently enough that the files of American and

British societies for psychical research are filled with hundreds of well-documented cases.

Each person's body and spirit, interacting in this manner under the tension that inheres to their different natures, gradually develop over a lifetime a spiritual character, with many values and intentions, some dominant and some less potent. This character, and not our stated goals or apparent ideals, determines the kind of spirit one will be in the totally spiritual life that follows physical death. Growth and development then, without the tension and capacity for change that characterizes our present dual existence, is slower and more difficult—if, indeed, we have not established so firmly committed a character that we are closed to future change.

This limitation on change of a person's essential character (more precisely, changing what Swedenborg calls one's "ruling love") should not be misunderstood as a restriction on eternal growth and development of the character one has formed during physical life. Continual growth toward infinite perfection of what one has chosen to be is an essential part of the vision of angelic existence.

People, Spirits, and Angels

This model of human personality, with its three spiritual components enveloped in a physical body, can aid our visualization of people living in physical and spiritual worlds simultaneously. Being a bridge between physical and spiritual reality, human beings are at home in both worlds to some extent and participate in both—though seldom equally.

The "absent-minded professor," to use an example so familiar that it may be trite, is so absorbed in spiritual/mental activities that the overlap of her consciousness with neural input concerning her physical environment is squeezed to almost nothing. Therefore, she is not conscious of the curbstone that her eye sees, and she trips over it and does other things that appear foolish to an observer who does not take into account her total concentration on unseen things. That same observer, however, with his feet solidly on the ground, might well become absorbed enough in reassembling a carburetor he has just cleaned that he ignores the feeling of warmth on the back of his neck and gets a painful sunburn. Examples such as the yogi in deep meditation or the league-leading hitter at the plate in a close game would illustrate greater extremes.

The variety of ways in which people's consciousness interacts with the spirit's two unconscious components makes it necessary to oversimplify when talking about people in general. However, it can be said that people have in their essential nature an inherent ability to perceive and respond to spiritual influences that is just as significant a part of their makeup as the parallel ability to perceive and respond to physical stimuli. When our body is in the room with the bodies of our friends, we interact with them physically. At the same time, however, our spirit is in the company of other spirits, interacting with them spiritually. The fact that we are more clearly conscious of physical interaction than the spiritual interaction does not diminish the reality of the spiritual contact or its effects on us.

There are times when, in that situation of simultaneous physical and spiritual companionship, the spiritual occupies a larger share of our consciousness than the physical. In a meeting that you have little interest in attending, for instance, the spiritual presence of another—a loved one, perhaps, thousands of miles away physically, but closer to you spiritually than the others in the room—may occupy your conscious mind so completely that you have to have a question repeated, even though your physical ear had heard the sounds perfectly well the first time.

Such an illustration shows the significant possibilities of our "double life." Many of those possibilities are never realized by most of us, because training, the example of mentors, and habit have caused us to all but eliminate the overlap of our consciousness and our spiritual perception. As noted, Swedenborg learned from angels that our earliest ancestors had been able to talk with spirits and angels as well as with people. In the course of generations long ago—while people were learning language, reflective thought, and other skills required to adapt to each other and their environment—they neglected their spiritual abilities to the point that many of those abilities were virtually lost. They passed on to succeeding generations, including our own, both their hard-won skills and their diminished spirituality. The spirituality is not lost from our essential makeup, however. It can be regained, with discipline, if it is sufficiently needed and desired.

A first step toward increased spiritual awareness is accepting and recognizing for what they are the spiritual influences now present in your life. One provision for guarding human freedom, discussed in the next chapter, is the ability to take personal credit (or blame, in some cases) for suggestions, inspirations, abilities, and guidance that actually come into our minds from spiritual sources. Our human ability to disguise and misinterpret spiritual forces in this way leaves us free to believe or not believe in spiritual reality.

If spiritual support and direction are accepted and recognized, and asked for without reservation (for example, without a covert hope that angels will help you get something that you want for other than heavenly reasons), spiritual or angelic help will come.

Asking God for help, guidance, strength, or anything else is called praying, of course; and praying to God is the best way to seek spiritual assistance. Angels act to achieve God's purposes and not necessarily to meet our goals. Swedenborg, who prayed a lot and had extraordinary awareness of spiritual processes, has this to say about prayer and its answer in his *Arcana Coelestia* (2535):

> Prayer, regarded in itself, is talking with God, and at the same time seeing the matters of the prayer in a spiritual perspective. This is answered with something like an influx into the perception or thought of the mind, so that there is a certain opening of the person's interiors toward God. This occurs differently according to the state of the person who is praying, and according to the essence of the subject of the prayer. If a person prays from love and faith, and for only heavenly and spiritual things, there then comes forth in the prayer something like a revelation (which is felt in the affection of the one who prays) as to hope, consolation, or a certain inward joy.

If the very act of praying focuses the mind on the spiritual aspects of what we're praying for, we have made the necessary first step toward getting an answer to prayer. Then, if we do not wait for a verbal answer but remain open to new feelings and subsequent changes in our approach to the matter, we experience some of the normal influence that angels can have on our lives. It usually is not something so obvious that it cannot be missed, but neither is it so hidden that it cannot be noticed. It is a subtle inner feeling that eventually becomes a new idea, ability, or solution (or whatever seemed out of reach before).

The appearance of angels in dreams and meditative states like those recounted in chapter 1 seems to be another kind of answer to prayer or an extension of the kind just described. Such appearances, or apparitions interrupting some fully conscious activity, can come in response to prayer, although sometimes with a delay; and I believe they can occur in response to prayers that were not consciously spoken— aloud or silently. Also, as was explained earlier in this chapter, angels can break into our consciousness uninvited, when the spiritual need is urgent enough.

How Angels Live

To say that angels and spirits are in the company of human spirits does not imply that angels sit around on our shoulders or stand quietly in some corner of our rooms. Angels and spirits are active with their own concerns, turning deliberately toward us only under special circumstances and for divine purposes. Much angelic influence, such as the normal answers to prayers, comes from the human spirit being in the presence of angels with similar purposes and intentions and absorbing from God though them the direction, or the power, or whatever is needed as an answer to prayer.

Angels live in homes as they did during their physical life, except that their homes are more perfect: there are no dangling gutters, peeling paint, or unkempt lawns. They wear clothes, which fit perfectly, and they wear a different style or color according to their mood or their state of mind. They go to work at their occupations, doing what they most love to do, enjoy a variety of recreational activities, and rest when they need to.

The reason for this similarity between angels' environment and activities and their lives in this world is an important one, and reflects one of the most significant principles that Swedenborg learned in his years of experience with the angels.

All that we see and know in this physical world—not just everything in general, but every single thing—is related to something in the spiritual world. The relationship is such that physical things draw their nature and appearance from their spiritual counterpart, and not the other way around. Horses, trees, rainbows, and other components of the natural or created order reflect primary elements of ideas and feelings. Sports cars, voting machines, television commercials, and other things that people make are projections of the spiritual condition and purpose of their maker. Angels are not spiritual projections of people; rather people are like angels and have the form of angels. Every naturally created thing derives its physical properties from the qualities of the spiritual reality to which it corresponds.

Correspondence is Swedenborg's term for this whole comprehensive spiritual-physical relationship, in which every physical object represents a spiritual one; and he saw correspondence as an essential key to understanding both the physical and spiritual worlds. In explaining the principle as it affects our understanding of angels, I will follow his usage in employing the same word in two other senses, which are closely related but distinguishable from this general one. *Correspondence,* or *correspondent,* is used also to describe a physical thing that truly represents a spiritual thing. This distinction is necessary because, while everything in this world—natural or manufactured—represents something spiritual, some human products appear to represent something, but their representation is deceptive in some way. A third usage is not as prominent in this book as in Swedenborg's works: everything in the Bible is a perfect representation of something spiritual, so Swedenborg's method of biblical interpretation is centrally concerned with defining biblical correspondences.

The correspondential relationship is a common element in the pattern of relationships that we call knowledge—so common that some effort may be required to recognize it. Whenever we meet other people, we notice the expression on their face. This expression, along with a number of less obvious clues that we call "body language," is recognized as a representation of qualities within the person. From people's expressions we can know something about their state of mind, their attitude toward us, and other things—if their expression honestly represents their attitude and feelings.

We have learned from experience that facial expressions do not always correspond to real feelings, but we know they represent what the person wants us to believe is going on inside; and we are accustomed to dealing with people on this basis.

We use this representational way of thinking in many other areas as well. When we consider a purchase, such as a new car, we compare its price with its worth in terms of the period of work that it represents to us. We think of an insurance policy as representing security for loved ones, of tilled rows of earth (with seed packets staked at the ends) as representing fresh vegetables on our table in a few weeks. We are thoroughly in the habit of valuing things for their inner meaning or potential. The principle of correspondence is simply a formulation of this way of thinking, as applied to the relationship between physical and spiritual things.

Water, for one example, is refreshing, cleansing, essential for life, virtually incompressible, and in other ways similar to truth; and indeed physical water corresponds to spiritual truth. The solid stability of the stones in a foundation derives from the same quality that we find in faith, to which they correspond. Different animals reflect our feelings about things and people: the useful ones, such as horses, representing a fondness for helping others, and lions and other feral stalkers corresponding to anger and hatred.

More abstract examples can be found in the correspondence of space and time to their spiritual counterparts. Distances between things or people are like differences between them, so we speak of things being "nearly" the same, or we feel "close" to someone whether or not we are in physical proximity. The parallels occur to us because physical space corresponds to spiritual "state" (as in "state of mind"), and distance corresponds to difference. Similarly, physical time corresponds to changes of state in the spiritual world, where there is no space or time as we know them. Water and rocks, horse and lions, space and time, all can be said to *correspond* to spiritual things because they are true representations. Possessions, on the other hand, represent good and helpful things that people have done for other individuals or the community, but do not necessarily *correspond*, because "ill-gotten gains" are indistinguishable in appearance from "well-gotten" ones.

In the spiritual world, however, there are no deceptive representations, only correspondences. Therefore an angel's house and its furnishings truly reflect the goodness of her or his deeds and motives. An angel's clothes correspond to his or her intelligence; and, since angels' intelligence increases and decreases as their love for others waxes and wanes, they wear clothes of different colors as these changes occur, brighter colors signifying higher intelligence.

Every single detail of angels' environment exists in correspondence, whether the detail is the location of their home in relation to the homes of other angels, or the ornament on their endtable, or the color of the flowers in their garden. Just as physical people have houses, possessions, and occupations, which together represent their contributions to their community, angels have homes and lifestyles corresponding to the benefit they contribute to the spiritual world. And those contributions are in some way corollary to the intentions that they adopted during their physical lifetime.

Love and Marriage among the Angels

Many Christians are surprised at the idea of angels being married, because they have understood Jesus's words in Matt. 22:30 (also Mark 12:25 and Luke 20:34-35) to mean that angels live in eternal celibacy. Swedenborg learned, however, that angels are bonded together in marriage love; and that Jesus's saying meant that heaven knows no weddings like those on earth, which involve bonding of flesh as well as spirit—and which include arranged marriages (for political, financial, or other extraneous considerations), marriage of convenience, and "shotgun weddings." Swedenborg points out Jesus's other teaching on marriage, recorded in Matt. 19 and Mark 10, in which he reaffirms the doctrine from Genesis, that a married couple are "no longer two, but one." Humans who become as one during their physical life continue to live spiritually as one after bodily death. Angels think and live with their spouses as one person. Those from the higher heavens, who have the more perfect marriages, appear from a distance as if they were just one angel.

Equality is a prominent aspect of this heavenly being-as-one called marriage. Any interest by either partner in controlling or dominating the other in any way would destroy true marriage love. Of course, spirits with a desire to dominate others would not be angels in the first place, so they would not be married to an angel. Angels marry only angels in their own community, which is made up of angels with

In heavenly marriage, two truly become one.

similar goals and values. What both angelic spouses intend, and what each enjoys most, is belonging to the other mutually and reciprocally.

The essence of heavenly marriage lies in uniting true discernment with good intention, so that the two become one. Swedenborg found that masculine spirits are most focused on thought, or discernment, and feminine spirits on affection, or intention; and that physical men and women correspond to this distinction—although men and women alike enjoy both faculties. Human marriages, therefore, join both the masculine and feminine spiritual qualities and the male and female physical qualities into one flesh in the physical world. If the couple also becomes spiritually one during their physical life, their marriage continues in heaven. Men and women who do not marry, or who become spiritually separated from their spouse, find truly compatible mates in their heavenly communities.

Heavenly marriage is part of the most sublime of all correspondential relationships. Just as the wedding of a physical couple in an earthly marriage corresponds to the bonding of discernment and intention in heaven, the heavenly marriage, in turn, corresponds to the union of divine wisdom and divine love in God. At a time when Europeans generally saw marriage as primarily a civil matter, Swedenborg's experiences in heaven led him to see worldly marriage as an essentially holy act, deriving its sanctity from his heavenly and divine correspondences. He tells how he learned from an angel that two humans who become joined in their minds to think as one form a correspondent, or image, of two angels in a heavenly marriage. Furthermore, since the heavenly marriage is an image of God, the human marriage also offers an image—although a less clear image—of the God of heaven and earth.

At the same time, men and women who are united in a false idea, particularly one arising from an evil intention, may have a passionate sexual attraction to each other, and may speak and act civilly toward each other; but their dominant relationship with one another is one of hatred rather than of love. Such couples correspond to the union of two spirits in hell, rather than to the union of angels in heaven.

One of Swedenborg's later works, originally published in Latin in 1768 and usually known in English as *Conjugial Love,* includes descriptions of many varieties of heavenly love and marriage, as well as a detailed account of the multi-level correspondence of the ideal marriage relationship. Swedenborg says that he learned that all the angels in heaven live in a state of true marriage love. Angels' married life is a significant component of the rich happiness called heavenly joy.

5. Freedom

Chapter 4 suggested an image of human life as a battleground on which both good and evil spirits struggle to gain greater influence over our lives. When military forces prepare for physical wars, they expend vast amounts of money and energy to learn as much as they can about the strengths and weaknesses of their allies as well as of their enemies, and they study the geography of the battlefield in detail. Analogously, a clearer perception of good and evil forces and the nature of the "battleground" will aid our efforts in our own personal battle.

First, a grammatical point needs to be made clear. While the words *good* and *evil* can be read as nouns, in this book they are generally used as adjectives. In the last paragraph, they were used to describe spirits; in other passages, they describe feelings, intentions, or actions. When they appear alone, as in "the good," or "what is good," the reference is to everything that can be described as good. What makes the distinction important is that here the discussion is focused on specific things that we can want or intend or do. Great, global abstractions are not the subject.

Second, a semantic point: all the "good" things or the "evil" or "bad" things being discussed are relatively good or bad. There are, no doubt, desires and actions that are absolutely good or evil, but few if any of us ever get involved with them. The battles we actually engage in concern choices in which one alternative is better than the other.

This relativity has a major effect on the nature of the battlefield. Visualize the battle as a kind of tug-of-war, in which we hold the center of a rope that is being pulled in each direction by opposing spirits. There is no centerline that, if crossed, marks victory for one side. Neither is there any likelihood of our being pulled across the endlines of the field. Instead, the rope is pulled by equally powerful forces so well balanced that a shift of our weight or effort makes a major difference, and the struggle moves back and forth across the field. Each decision that moves us toward what is good, for example, is a victory for the angels—even if the two alternatives were far toward the other end of the field. One person's action, chosen as an alternative to something more harmful, could be a good choice, while the same action, chosen by another person instead of a more constructive possibility, could be evil.

What makes an action good or evil is the direction or tendency of the choice in the context of an individual life. A tendency toward God makes a choice good, and a tendency away from God makes it bad. A tendency toward God may be exemplified by a dependence on divine guidance in preference to human judgment, an intention that is in closer conformity with moral principles or a rejection of an impulse perceived as contrary to God's will.

Closely aligned with good and evil influences are true and false ones. The two pairs are distinguishable: the first involves our will, desires, values, intentions, and actions, while the second influences our intellectual faculty, reasoning, understanding, discernment, and analysis. Although there are exceptions that fascinate philosophers, good intentions usually are based on true perceptions, and vice versa. Certainly good intentions desire true perceptions, and malicious intentions relish distortions.

False and Evil Influences

In physical warfare (returning to that analogy), each side seeks total control of the other. However, wars seldom are fought by the entire forces of both sides, but rather by groups of individual soldiers fighting in some particular but usually insignificant place. Our spiritual battles are much the same. As angels on one side and devils (or evil spirits) on the other compete for dominant influence over our decisions, their conflict is reflected in our experience only in specific choices and actions that often seem too trivial to bother about—except that the cumulative effect of these decisions eventually forms our character as a good or bad person. This appearance, that some of our choices and decisions are not important and really do not matter very much, is a false one, used deceptively by evil spirits. They try in this way to incline us toward indulging a tempting desire without the consideration we might otherwise give it.

Unfortunately, the illusion of insignificance is not the only falsity by which evil spirits are able to help us deceive ourselves. Most of us also are open to their suggestion that spiritual forces have nothing to do with our decisions. This willingness on the part of many of us arises from the widespread conviction that our senses, together with our memories of sense data, provide all the influences that affect our minds. It is true, of course, that our senses and memories do

*Evil spirits, as well as angels, approach us through dreams
and the subconscious.*

influence the electrochemical processes in our brain that we
call thought. However, our common oversimplification involves an assumption that the words *good* and *evil* are only
labels that we assign to physical things that benefit or harm
us—that we are independent of any spiritual forces and that
there are no evil spirits, or any kind of spirits at all, actively
working to affect our thoughts and actions.

Most of us, at least among those who are willing to entertain the idea of spiritual influences, find it easier to believe that some evil force pushes us toward things considered wrong. We would rather take credit for making right
decisions on our own, but we have a natural proclivity for
shifting blame whenever possible. Consider the comment of
Paul in his letter to the Christians in Rome: "I do not do the
good I want, but the evil I do not want is what I do" (Rom.
7:19). The persistent and ingenious rationalizations that

keep coming to mind after we have decided against a tempting course of action feel so spontaneous that they seem to come from another source. The devious self-exemptions from principles that hold us back from our chosen course feel the same way. So, too, do the subtle enhancements that make it increasingly attractive as we "argue with ourselves" about it.

If we entertain—even only as an experiment—the idea that evil forces are pushing us towards evil actions, then the key to preserving our original good intention will be found in prayer for spiritual assistance, rather than in repeated attempts to stiffen our steadily fading resolve. If prayer works, in this admittedly uncontrolled experiment, at least the circumstantial evidence will point toward the reality of a spiritual struggle going on around or within us—a struggle in which our appeal for help from good spirits and angels is a decisive factor. If prayer helps us again, belief in spiritual influence will be reinforced. Recurrences of the same result in this universal human situation strongly support Swedenborg's report of what he observed from the spiritual perspective: our consciousness is a battlefield in which good and evil spirits compete, and our spiritually aware decision can determine the outcome.

What, exactly, are evil spirits? Simply stated, they are the souls of people who, in their physical life, chose false goals over true ones and bad actions over good ones. This pattern, intentionally repeated, causes these goals and actions to become their preference. In the spiritual world, their true selves revealed, they continue to prefer the same goals and do the same things. When our own thinking comes close enough to theirs, they use the perceptions and persuasions that have worked for them to influence us in their preferred direction. Since they work through our minds, they are just as clever at thinking up arguments against our good intentions as we can be at thinking up arguments favoring them. In effect, we are outnumbered in this battle, unless or until we ask God for help. If we do, sincerely and wholeheartedly, the odds are changed by the angels he sends to our aid, and the devils cannot win, as has been pointed out already. If we do not seek help, we pit our own moral strength alone against an unseen enemy whose power we cannot judge. Under these conditions, evil often wins.

Equilibrium

A description of the role of angels in the spiritual equilibrium that preserves human freedom requires a little more background. Two of the appearances that contribute to the popular illusion that spirituality is unimportant or nonexistent have been mentioned already—the apparent triviality of decisions that really are important and the suspicion that spiritual influences have no effect. There is another to look at, one which has been debated both by the greatest minds in western civilization and by sophomore philosophy classes, and which still impedes common sense. Theologians sometimes call it the Problem of Evil (as if evil were not enough of a problem in the first place), and it surfaces in philosophy classes in the form of such profundities as "If God is good, he can't be god; and if God is god, he can't be good." In

God maintains equilibrium between good and evil.

short, why does a loving God permit war, famine, hatred, genocide, and all the rest?

The problem in this "problem of evil" appears overwhelming, and in the terms and assumptions of some formulations, it is entirely insoluble. However, there is more than one way of looking at the issue. Swedenborg's approach includes a concept of freedom of choice, ordained by God in the created nature of human beings. As we will see, freedom of choice is the key element in our human ability to deal with the spiritual forces around us, and it is preserved inviolate by God. The divine mechanism for preserving this freedom is the equilibrium that is maintained between opposing forces—true influences vs. false ones, forces attracting us to good motives and actions vs. forces attracting us to evil and harm.

Under these conditions, the spiritual struggle between good and evil within each human being continues throughout life. That is the "bad news." But the good news is that every battle in this war can be won by our decision to rely on the spiritual resources, the angels around us. In fact, there are a few people who do choose angelic guidance and support so consistently that it becomes their habitual and characteristic response to every situation. For them, it is as if the battle were over. Swedenborg saw angels guarding people like this, and described it this way in *Arcana Coelestia* (50):

> The angels [then] rule, and inspire them with all goods and truths, and with fear and horror of evils and falsities. The angels indeed lead, but only as ministers, for it is the Lord alone who governs people through angels and spirits.

Most of us have known people who illustrate this condition. Usually, they are older people, men or women who have survived enough challenges in life to have settled a lot of issues for themselves, whether they talk about their experiences or not. They are people it feels good to be with. They make you think, as you consider them, "I hope someday I can . . . " Mother Teresa is one example, but the most vivid illustrations will come from each person's own experience.

Guardian Angels

Angels are with people throughout human life. Their presence with infants has been described already. As a child grows and matures, these early guardians are replaced by angels who are best prepared by their own human experience to understand and assist with the problems of that particular individual at each stage of his or her development. Acting as

Angels watch over us throughout our life.

supporters now, rather than guardians as before (that is, before the infants had the ability to reason or the freedom that arises from it), these angels do everything possible to suggest right choices and encourage good intentions, exerting as much influence on our perceptions and our feelings as we will freely accept. No matter how far we have followed evil spirits down self-destructive paths, angels keep trying. Their work is the heavenly implementation (parallel to God's direct influence) of the infinite divine mercy.

When people let physical desires drive their intentions and actions until this becomes their normal pattern, angels suggest something good that they can do in response to these urges. People who habitually make up their minds on the basis of false values related only to their personal pleasure will be led by angelic influence to think of higher values that also give pleasure. To preserve each individual's freedom, these suggestions never enter our mind in the form of clear knowledge or absolute certainty. They appear in consciousness as possibilities, as questions: for instance, in the form "I wonder if . . ." People can reject the suggestions, act against the advice, ignore the presence of angels and spirits, and even deny their existence. For the sake of human freedom, angels do not enforce their guidance.

Angelic gentleness, subtlety, and respect for our freedom to choose should not be allowed to dim our understanding of the power of our guarding or guiding angels, nor lead us to underestimate their significance in our lives. Their vital importance to us was seen clearly by Swedenborg when he observed what angels and spirits do for people. He states in *Arcana Coelestia* (50):

> By spirits human beings have communication with the world of spirits, and through angels with heaven. Without communication by means of spirits with the world of spirits, and by means of angels with heaven, and thus through heaven with [God], people could not live at all. Our life entirely depends on this conjunction, so that if the spirits and angels were to withdraw, we would instantly perish.

This is another way of saying that God maintains and sustains us during every living moment. Angels provide the medium that modulates the infinite power of divine love into a life force on our human order of magnitude. But it is not only the general power to exist that angels give us. In *Heaven and Hell* (228), Swedenborg tells how

Angels have been permitted to move my steps, my actions, and my tongue and speech, as they pleased, and this by influx into my will and thought; and I have learned thereby that of myself I could do nothing. I was afterwards told by them that everyone is so ruled, and that we can know this from the doctrine of the church and from the Word. People pray that God may send angels to lead them, direct their steps, teach them, and inspire in them what to think and what to say, and other like things; although they say and believe otherwise when they are thinking by themselves apart from the teaching of the church.

Sometimes worldly or bodily setbacks—even calamities—interrupt the angels' leading, direction, teaching and inspiration. Instinct may urge us, when that happens, to rely on our own experience and courage to get things back to normal. The angelic counsel conveyed by Swedenborg calls for more earnest prayer and dependence on angelic support during such reversals.

Swedenborg learned from experience that angels have power that humans can hardly imagine in a being. The Bible describes the power of angels, telling of the cherub with the flaming sword who prevented Adam and Eve from returning to Eden, the fiery chariot and horses that bore Elijah to heaven (II Kings 2:11), and many other fearsome instances. But in spite of this strength and this intimate involvement with our lives, angels restrain their influence over us so that we never are dominated by it. One example of the many ways in which angels can intervene on our behalf, without abridging our freedom, can be drawn from my own recent experience.

As I was falling asleep one night, unwanted fantasies and thoughts crowded out what I had been thinking. Feeling too tired and off guard to resist them, I entertained them as I fell asleep. In a dream, I climbed steep stairs or a ladder into a dimly lit attic or loft. Noticing some movement in one corner of the space, I went closer to investigate. As I approached, a creature climbed down from some kind of a shelflike perch onto the same level as I was. The thing did not frighten me so much as it revolted me. It seemed coarse-skinned, leathery; its arms and legs (or forelegs and hindlegs—it seemed humanlike, but also inhuman) were about equal in length and rather long for its body. Its face, also ambiguously human, displayed beady eyes and big teeth in a mouth spread into a grin or a grimace. The features were close set in a large face.

The thing was not aggressive or threatening, nor was it afraid of me. It moved slowly but appeared to be very strong. I imagined trying to kill it but saw that I would not be nearly strong enough. We stared at each other, I with loathing for it, and it (I thought) with contempt for me. Nothing happened, but presently I woke in distress, my heart pounding.

I had not been asleep long before the dream, and soon fell asleep again afterwards, more soundly. But as I was dozing off, my horror at this creature fully occupied my mind, completely crowding out the unwanted fantasies that had been so persistent before. The next morning, my vivid recollection of the dream led me to realize that the creature had been a kind of representation of the evil spirits that kept dragging me into these scenarios and tempting me to enjoy them. Over time, it or he had grown too strong for me to destroy by my own strength, and it seemed sure enough of eventual victory that it could afford to be patient. My feeling, as I thought this, was that angels had warned me about the nature of my adversary by letting me see it. They were guarding me against underestimating the opposition. The warning itself served to free me from its influence for a while, but the message of the dream was that the struggle was far from over.

I should have known this in any case, because that particular struggle had been going on for years. Later in this chapter, there is a description of one of my (rather, the angels' and my) major victories; yet despite that and others, the battle continues. I have sought and received spiritual assistance in this spiritual conflict, but have not yet accepted angelic guidance completely.

I have no doubt that the influence of angels is always sufficient to preserve a perfect equilibrium with the power of evil spirits, but that influence is never so great that I cannot resist it, ignore it, or deny to myself that it even exists. In this, I believe that I am Everyone, fighting a battle I cannot win alone. I am protected from losing so long as I trust my protector, but still am unable or unwilling to surrender to my protector, though I would then be victorious. It is a difficult situation, yet one that is inherently hopeful, to be kept free this way by equilibrium.

Whom Do We Trust?

The self-restraint of angels in their influence over us is a necessary condition for the preservation of our freedom to choose for ourselves between what is right and what is wrong, and similarly between what is good and what is bad. This restraint provides an explanation for the diversity of informed opinion about the existence of angels. Some people have welcomed the presence and assistance of angels and have felt this attitude rewarded often enough that they no longer doubt the existence of angelic and spiritual companionship and support. Such people find their instinctive interpretations and intentions gradually changing. As this change progresses, they become more and more like angels, so that they are able to enjoy occasional conscious contact with their spiritual community—hearing or seeing angels in dreams or times of meditation—without their freedom being threatened by the experience. On the other hand, those who deny the existence of spiritual beings or spiritual influences on their lives might be compelled to believe if an angel appeared to them. So, under most circumstances, angelic appearances do not happen to them.

When you hear people tell you that they have seen an angel, or an angel has done this or that for them, your own experience and knowledge of that person may predispose you either to believe them or to doubt them: human experience is not consistent on this point. The same circumstance affects your inclination to accept or reject the opinions of people who are convinced that angels have no existence outside of overactive imaginations.

We choose what to believe and whom to trust.

This book and others like it—or books on the other side of the fence—may confirm your experience or contradict it. It is likely that most books exploring spiritual matters will harmonize with some of your experiences and conflict with others. No proof is going to appear, on one side or the other, that is going to demonstrate the existence or nonexistence of angels beyond all reasonable doubt. God and the whole heaven of angels conspire continually to preserve the equilibrium that keeps that from happening. You always remain free to believe in angels and trust them to aid you when you call, and equally free to ignore or deny their existence and depend solely on your own strength and judgment.

The responsibility of reaching your own conclusion in matters of faith, as in all others, is inherent in the freedom of choice that is characteristic of human nature. Deciding to suspend judgment is itself a decision, so the responsibility cannot be avoided or long postponed. Everyone is forced to decide what to believe and whom to trust.

Spiritual equilibrium does not, however, restrict angels and spirits from providing aid that is freely sought. This includes assistance in deciding whether to believe in or trust them. While they do not provide irrefutable evidence, angels do offer experiences that are convincing to anyone who really wants to believe.

A friend of mine who did not believe in angels and strongly doubted the existence of God found herself in a period of deep depression and extremely anxious uncertainty. She did not know what to do and doubted her ability to carry out any plan she might decide on. Another friend suggested to her that she try asking for help, regardless of whether or not she believed that anyone was there to ask. Highly skeptical, but with a willingness formed out of desperation, she lay on her bed one evening and "asked the empty room" for help. Almost immediately, a feeling of peace seemed to spread over her "like a warm blanket," and she was able to sleep. Awaking the next morning, she saw clearly the next step for her to take and felt confident of her ability to take it. Now, years later, her trust in God and in spiritual power is as sure an assumption about her environment as her confidence that the next step will support her when she walks down stairs.

Another example from my own experience involves a night of deep despair, when I lay awake in the hours between midnight and dawn (as dark to my mind's eye as to my wide-open physical eyes), endlessly replaying unwanted fantasies that I could not exorcise from my consciousness. The thought occurred to me that I should pray, so I started silently to repeat the Lord's Prayer. After a phrase or two, I became reabsorbed in the fantasies and lost the thought of praying. Eventually recalling my purpose, I started again with the same result. After failing a third time, I experienced a horrible sinking feeling and a painful knot in my stomach, as I realized that the fantasies had control of me, and I could not pray!

In fearful panic, I cried, almost aloud (but not quite, since my wife was sleeping beside me), "Lord, help me! Help me pray." By the time I had thought the words, my body relaxed, with a feeling that helps me understand what my friend said about the warm blanket. Beside my bed, close enough that I could have touched him if I had reached out my hand, my father was standing, waiting to pray with me. He had been dead for over a decade, but that did not occur to me at the time, or seem relevant if it did. Also, it was only in retrospect that I realize that he and I had never prayed together, except sitting in the same pew at church or at the Sunday dinner table. Although I did not open my eyes, I knew he was there: I even knew his posture and how he was dressed.

I repeated the Lord's Prayer to myself slowly and with full concentration, finding rich, fresh meanings in the words. Then I prayed for the specific help I needed at the time, falling asleep at the end. The attitude with which I rose in the morning, including a new perspective on my problems and a determination to act differently than I had been acting, was a direct answer to my prayers. That determination persisted for months, until the new behavior had become habitual. There was nothing overpowering about it. I suspect I could have turned my father's presence into an illusion by simply opening my eyes (almost consciously, I realized that at the time). However, I chose to accept his spiritual presence, and I received the support I needed.

Putting it another way, I trusted the God I had prayed to more than I trusted my own judgments, which had gotten me into the situation. I trusted the spirit sent in answer to my prayer more than I trusted my physical perceptions. In my personal interpretation of what happened, I feel certain that it was the trust that enabled me to benefit from the spiritual experience.

Who's in Charge?

There is an important question that has not been explicitly stated here, but might appear to have been answered in two or three different ways in the various contexts in which it has been implied. That is the question of who really "calls the shots" as we live our lives, making choices, acting spontaneously or deliberately. I have stated that we ourselves do, as we exert our divinely protected freedom to make choices. It could be inferred from the previous discussion that angels and spirits do, by means of the help they give or appear to withhold. Finally, it should be clear that God directs angels, spirits, and humans, as God continuously provides for their

God directs angels, spirits, and humans.

personal and collective growth and well-being. Who, really, is in charge?

In some sense, each of the three views has some truth; but a useful understanding of our ongoing relationship with angels requires clear knowledge of the relationship between those truths. The primary truth, in the light of which the others can be true and without which they are false and dangerously misleading, is that God provides all the power enabling angels, spirits, and human beings to do anything—even to exist. In this sense, both fundamental and supreme, God alone is "in charge." God alone is the author of history. The apparent autonomy that we feel in our own decision-making and that we seem to see in others is a function of the freedom of choice with which God has equipped all human creatures.

Angels see the relationship between divine power and individual freedom more directly than people do. In the light of heaven, there are far fewer illusions than appear in physical light, so angels are fully aware that their every breath, thought, and action is enabled solely by God. But even with this angelic perception, angels must make choices as if they depended on their ability alone. We human beings, whose perceptions are clouded by the ambiguities of physical existence, are faced with the necessity of acting as if we had complete free will, with our radical dependence on God only a theory—for some, a theory supported by faith. If we fail to resolve the freedom/dependence dilemma on a personal level, surrender to either side can prove disastrous. We are like Ulysses, steering between Scylla and Charybdis. If we recognize our dependence on God but neglect our concomitant liberty, we are left immobile and without direction. If we avoid that pitfall by giving it too wide a berth, we are ensnared by its opposite, hyperactivity without any direction except our own, wildly gyrating compass.

It is a law of life, if not of logic, that the only real solution to a true dilemma is a genuine paradox. A paradox is a statement of opposites, both of which are true. The paradox of freedom—that freedom is a necessary illusion that provides our only access to the empowerment that is found in our total dependence on God—may, like all paradoxes, be impossible to accept on rational terms. However, thinking and acting as if it were true can provide pragmatic evidence of its validity. In simplest terms: if we act as if there were no help from heaven, while we pray as if there were no help on earth, our life works better than if we rely too heavily on either alternative.

6. *What We Can Do*

What does a person who knows about angels and spirits do differently from one who does not know about them? That is a central issue, because our ability to know about angels (to know, as opposed to reading and theorizing) is greatly affected by our motive for wanting to know. Angels, after all, are the best teachers about the nature and work of angels; and angels respond to requests that conform to their values and purposes.

If you want to know about angels to satisfy your curiosity, real angels are not aware of your desire. Instead, spirits who in their physical existence were absorbed in odd facts and peculiar trivia are more likely to respond, and they will let you know the kinds of things that intrigue your curiosity, whether the things are relevant or not, or even true. If you are a man interested in angels because you are intrigued by images of shapely women in gauzy robes, any response you get would likely come from male spirits who used to collect pictures in some secret hiding place, or from feminine spirits who, as humans, enjoyed dressing provocatively to intrigue men.

If you want to learn how to find the willpower, or the wisdom, to do something for someone who really needs your help, then your search is more likely to attract the attention of angels, particularly the ones already seeking a way to aid the same person. Angels look for ways to help that do not impede the needful person's freedom to believe or not believe in angels—a "way" just like you, offering to help.

It is what we want to do with our knowledge, and more especially what we have done with the knowledge we have, that determines our access to real knowledge of angels. If we want to do things that are good for other people, do them for the others' sake more than for our own, and (like the king's faithful steward in the gospel story [Matt. 25:14-30]) use the knowledge that we already have to help others, we are in a spiritual position to learn more.

Generalities like this, of course, ignore the diversity, the intensely personal individuality, of the decisions and actions that open us to knowing more about angels. Understanding of our inner motivations requires practiced introspection and quite possibly the aid of a counselor or spiritual director as well; a book like this can point only in the most general direction. Recognizing those limitations, however, there are some things to say about using a knowledge of angels

We Can Help People

Perhaps the surest way to gain a personal acquaintance with angels is to invite angelic participation in our activities by praying for their assistance in an attempt to help someone. However, that statement presupposes a particular understanding of the role that our motives play in our spiritual relationships. Concern for ourselves connects us with selfish spirits, so endeavoring to help a friend for the purpose of enjoying the experience of angelic assistance in our effort would tend to separate us from the angels rather than to draw them near us. On the other hand, a request for health or strength or emotional stability for ourselves, so that we might be able to aid someone, would draw us closer to angelic associations.

The difference between the two examples lies in the reasons that instigate the two intentions more than in the nature or substance of the intentions themselves. This may be obvious, but it is important enough to be developed further. Every action we intend to carry out has several layers of motivation. We can attempt to assist someone because we are motivated by a concern for their well-being or because we want to be thought of as a nice person. We may seek election to an office that lends us some prestige because we enjoy being looked up to or because we can help more people if we have the office than if we do not. From the angels' perspective, it is the motive at the bottom of these various layers, the deepest motivation, that is most significant. They are attracted to or repelled by us on the basis of our most fundamental goals—purposes that we may not admit, even to ourselves in our conscious thinking.

Therefore, it takes an interest in helping someone else for his or her own sake, or at least for the sake of being able to be happy about that person's happiness, to attract angelic companionship; and it is only when our best efforts fall short of our intentions that angelic companions suggest new ways or increase our strength. But if our most interior motive is directed toward the benefit of others, and the obstacles are great enough, angels do come to our aid. They come in many other circumstances as well—some that we can understand

Concern for others connects us with angels.

and some that we cannot—but their desire to help is so strong that this is the context in which we are most likely to experience their presence.

The desire on our part to be useful to someone else may be much more specific in the angels' sight than in ours. For example, a friend of mine who is a pastor tells the following story. After putting his family in the car to go to church one Sunday, he felt behind schedule as usual. Backing out of his driveway, he heard a voice as clearly as if it were one of the children's saying, "Your sermon is on your desk." Certain that he had put his sermon for that morning in his briefcase, he wondered about the voice for a moment and then decided to go on. However, the seemingly audible warning was repeated. Feeling annoyed and foolish, he dashed back into the house, looked at his desk—and saw the sermon lying there!

Reflecting on the event, he thought of his brother, who had died in childhood and who seemed to have warned him of danger at other times; but he could not clearly recognize the voice he had heard and was surprised to find so much spiritual significance attached to the typescript of his sermon. Someone in the congregation may have had an urgent need to hear in his sermon that morning something he might have forgotten to say if he had forgotten his manuscript. Perhaps there was another reason, known only to the angels. But there was a "bottom line": the intention that had motivated his work on that sermon would have had no effect without spiritual intervention, and something in that intention was of spiritual significance to one of his listeners—

enough significance to prompt some angel or spirit to act. Saving my friend the embarrassment of getting up in the pulpit without his sermon was a fortunate by-product, but probably not of sufficient spiritual gravity to have prompted the voice that he heard.

Another friend, also a pastor, has told me of an event in which angelic participation was so subtle that no one noticed it. Fresh out of the seminary, he had arrived in the city of his first pastorate just after the death of a prominent member of his congregation. Calling on the family of the deceased, motivated much more by a desire to be of help than by a knowledge of anything he could do to help, he found a large group of relatives and close friends gathered to mourn their loss. He felt overwhelmingly inadequate to the situation, so he shook hands with everyone as he was introduced, saying as little as possible; and then sat on a chair, watching everyone but saying nothing, until he felt he had been there long enough. As he left the house, he felt certain that he had failed his first pastoral test.

In due time, he conducted the funeral, receiving words of appreciation afterwards but still feeling he had let the church and the family down to some extent. In later years, however, friends of that family told him of having heard how wise and how comforting he had been on that occasion when he had first come to town. My friend was told how much the family had appreciated what he had said and how they had advised others to have confidence in this young minister who was so strong a rock in time of trouble.

He told that story to me, and probably to other young ministers as well, to illustrate the importance of "being there" to comfort people, even when uncertain what to say. What he left untold, because he could not know with certainty, is who put into the minds of those family members the things that they remembered hearing from him. People who might not have been willing (or might not have been able, while remaining free to choose) to hear the voice of an angel, were able to remember hearing and feeling angelic comfort—so long as they could attribute the memory to their pastor, whose presence and spiritual intention could be used by angels in their ministering purpose.

My own experience of the last few years has taught me a good deal about the quiet kind of spiritual or angelic activity in my life, the kind that provides no dramatic stories but that provides support that has no other source or explanation. My wife has been afflicted with a progressive condition that appears to be either an atypical Alzheimer's disease or an Alzheimer's-related disease, which has deprived her of most of her ability to communicate verbally (by speaking or writing), and of many manual skills as well. Although I have considered myself a caring person who tries to be helpful, I was as unprepared as most (I suppose) for a role as caretaker. The expanding and shifting "job description" for that role has presented mental, emotional, and spiritual challenges that quickly exhausted the resources of my education and experience.

The realization that I needed to pray for support in order to cope with my situation came slowly. I was too busy trying to solve problems and calm my emotions to reflect objectively on what was happening. When I did pray about these things, I remembered the depths of despair from which I had prayed before and how help had come in response. After that, I began trying to solve fewer of my problems on my own and offering more of them in prayer (though continuing distractions from minor but immediate crises kept diffusing my attention). Slowly, although certainly not steadily, changes appeared.

By now, I have ceased to be surprised (most of the time) at the caretaking skills and attitudes I am able to develop without a visible teacher, and I seldom wonder any more how I am going to handle the progressive worsening of my wife's condition. It is not that I know how I will do so, but that I know I will do so, somehow. The tasks that I had not been able to keep up with have gotten done, with slivers of time left over to write this book, which may help someone, too.

Most important of all to me, my sadness over the lost abilities that frustrate my wife so much has not spread to any particular sadness or self-pity related to the things I do for her. Instead, I have come to find a contentment that includes moments close to joy—a state of mind and spirit that I had not imagined, let alone prayed for. My religious faith, which at first seemed challenged in my circumstances, is stronger than ever. My trust in the dependability of spiritual support has been confirmed beyond question. I could not have managed this without help, and with the same assurance as I have that the sun will set tonight, I know that the help came from angels. It came, I think, partly because I prayed and partly because, by assisting me, the angels could help my wife, who most needs their angelic care.

No one supposes that when Jesus commanded his followers to love one another (John 15:17), he referred to harboring some vague romantic feeling about other people. More clear in New Testament Greek than in translation, his *agapate allelous,* "love one another," directs us to give—freely and happily—whatever benefits those around us. Angels enjoy giving in that way more than anything else, and humans who obey his commandment eventually find themselves in the fellowship of those angels.

We Can Keep in Touch

Another thing to do with a knowledge of angels is to keep in touch with them. This means making prayer and meditation, with a heavenly or angelic orientation, a habit having top priority in every day's activities. I hope that this is worded carefully enough, but more needs to be said about a fundamental ambiguity involved in advising anyone to pray.

For me and for many readers, this means praying to the risen and glorified Lord Jesus, the Christ. But these words mean different things to different Christians; and for many non-Christians, advice in the same spirit should be stated in very different words. One of the extremely important things that Swedenborg learned from seeing angels in action in their heavenly environment is that everyone on earth is able to

learn what is true or good from One that they call God—
even though they use different names for, and ascribe different attributes to, their God.

Individuals involved with any religion who habitually
practice their religion the best they know how are able to become angels of the universal heaven after their physical
death. All, including Christians, have an obligation to bear
witness by their actions to the God they know; but this
obligation, if it were separated from distinctions and con-
flicts of purely human invention, would lead to peaceful co-
operation among people of differing faiths, rather than to
the hostility that is so commonly seen. Christians, and all
others, can live more happily and fruitfully if they pray to
the God they know, if they accept and put to use the angelic
support provided them, and if they live their daily lives as an
expression of their faith or religion.

One of the reasons this works is that the practice of our
religion is more difficult than assent to its ideas, and people
who act out the dictates of their religion have done the most
important work of adopting it. Another reason, reported by
Swedenborg from his observations in the world of spirits, is
that spirits who, in their human life, had in fact practiced
their religion willingly and sometimes with joy are able to
learn easily any intellectual corrections that might be necessary to their religious understanding. Intentions and actions
are harder to change in the spiritual world than in the physical one we know, but thinking can be amended much more
easily in that environment. Most novitiate spirits, in the
process of developing the self-awareness that they need,

Daily prayer keeps us in touch with angels.

spend some "time" (or what feels like time in a realm where time as we measure it does not exist) in communities like schools, in which they clarify and correct their understandings of spiritual realities, especially of God.

We Can Help the Angels

There is a story set in the aftermath of World War II that is worth telling here. I have not checked its accuracy, but it has a mythic quality that conveys truth, whether or not the facts are straight. Workmen reconstructing Dresden, after the terrible bombing late in the war, found a statue of Jesus in the rubble. The figure was intact, except that both hands were broken off the ends of the outstretched arms. After much discussion, the burghers decided to put the statue on its pedestal as it was found, even though replacing the hands was a feasible option. Their reputed reasoning: the Christ needs hands to do his work on earth. The statue with broken stumps at the wrists would stand as a reminder to all who saw it that the Christ needs their hands.

In the spirit of that tale, create in your mind's eye a vision of a sweetly comforting angel, or a terrifying angel defending the truth, and imagine the figure without hands, waiting for you and your hands to complete its heavenly purpose. The image is not farfetched. A person who would shrug off the memory of an angel appearing in a dream and who would be compelled (not free to believe or not) if an angel appeared in the flesh, can be challenged, guided, or comforted, according to need, by an ordinary person acting on angelic prompting.

If we live as angels on earth, we receive heavenly joy.

This is, perhaps, another way of saying, "Help one another," as suggested above; or of saying, "Keep in touch" with the added injunction ". . . and pay attention!" It is both of those together, but something more, as well. As has been pointed out, helping someone for her sake, or his sake, brings you closer to the angels than helping someone for the sake of your own reputation. But there is a still higher motive, which places you in the company of angels even closer to God. You can help someone for God's sake—acting out a prayer that God make you a more effective helper, helping as an act of worship. Doing something good, for a purpose like that, teams you with high and powerful angels. In a memorable chapter in his book *Heaven and Hell* (530), Emanuel Swedenborg points out that

> Almost everyone practices honesty and fairness in outward matters. . . . The spiritual person needs to live the same way . . . the only difference being that the spiritual person . . . behaves honestly and fairly not just because it is in keeping with civil and moral laws, but because it is in keeping with divine laws. For people who are thinking about divine matters while they are active [in their daily affairs] are in touch with the angels of heaven . . . and bonded to them.

You cannot find better company, nor a more rewarding and satisfying life. In the end, this is the reason for knowing as much as you can about angels. If, in this world, you come as near as possible to living as angels live in heaven, you receive from them a priceless share of heavenly joy. This joy offers all the benefits of happiness, comfort, certainty, and elation on this earth.

Swedenborg knew heavenly joy from experience, but found it impossible to describe in detail. In *Heaven and Hell* (320), he explains:

> To enable me to know the nature and quality of heaven and heavenly joy, [God] has long and often granted me perception of the delightful qualities of heavenly joys. So I can know this because it comes from live experience; but I can never describe it. . . . I have perceived that joy and delight seem to come from the heart, spreading very gently through all the deepest fibers and from there into gathered fibers [of the sensory nervous system], with such a profound feeling of pleasure that the fibers are virtually nothing but joy and delight, with every derived perceptive and sensitive element alive with happiness. Next to these joys, the joys of physical pleasures are like coarse and acrid dust relative to a pure and very soft aura.

It is a gift that only God can give, and he gives it to his angels. People who live as angels live, acting from angelic motives, are living in material bodies while their spirits are in heaven. They are angels who are visible among us. While their appearance may not differ from the appearance of others, a little time spent in their presence is a cheering, encouraging experience. We can find people like that. We can be people like that. We can be angels in action, the kind of people who, Swedenborg says, "appear in heaven before the angels as beautiful human beings, and as their partners and companions."